The Secret Diary of a

SPICE

BOY

C000161687

The Secret Diary of a

SPICE

BOY

Making and Breaking the World's Biggest Music Exhibition

A self-published autobiography by

Alan Smith-Allison

Imprint: Independently published

First Published in 2019.

KDP ISBN 9781098608842

Contents

Introduction

Well it's been an incredible journey creating and travelling with the biggest Spice Girls' exhibition ever. There have been incredible highs and unbelievable lows, but as I take the chance to reflect on the journey and on life in general, it really has to be one of the highlights of my life. Follow your dreams, you will never regret giving it your best shot but will always regret not even trying.

To me, as well as millions of fans around the world, the Spice Girls were more than just a 90s pop group. They were a movement, a sign that times were changing and that it was okay to be unique and different from the crowd.

Nothing was ever too serious, how could it be when five girls were interviewing on a couch pinching each other, taking the mickey out of the presenter or pulling silly faces to camera. What was serious was the message behind it all.

> "Work hard, try hard and you can achieve anything and be anybody you want to be."

> "Don't be afraid to be different, be yourself

and do what makes you happy."

I could write another twenty empowering quotes from them that really impacted on my thinking and my life.

The Spice Girls virtually held my hand and told me to believe in myself. I was never alone when they were around and I am so glad I got the opportunity to grow up with them as my distant mentors.

Thank you ladies, you really did change my life!

1

It Makes You Wanna Zig Ah Zig Ahhh

I had always dreamt of having some kind of exhibition or show with the collection from the moment I bought my first costume piece from Mel B's 2007 Clic Sargent sale. I instantly wanted it to be in a display cabinet and on show in a museum somewhere. I often wonder if this is the sale where costume collecting really became accessible for the fans. Melanie sold off most of her Spice Girls' wardrobe (rather like Geri had done previously in 1998 but in a more affordable and accessible way. Geri had a Sotheby's sale that not everyone could access in the 90s but the Mel B sale was on eBay and was available worldwide), not only her wardrobe but most of the contents of her house as well. I bought loads of stuff from candlesticks to ashtrays and of course that all important first ever costume piece, Mel B's very own Pepsi costume.

The Pepsi costume is, in itself, a story that Spice fans won't like and, as I look back at it, it is a little cringe worthy. I wasn't sure at that point if I was going to be able to afford to collect Spice Girls' costumes and even although I went on an immediate search around online for others, I was also a bit skint (broke, poor, cashless) and had the grand idea of trying to sell the costume on. The problem was, even though I was skint, I loved the costume so much from the moment it arrived. The feel of it, the brightness of the Pepsi print all over it, how bold it was, how tiny, how typically Scary Spice, it had a unique smell to it as soon as I unwrapped it and it was made of wet suit style material, I remember being really emotional about it. I was holding one of my idol's iconic stage costumes, I'd waited and longed for a costume piece for so long, how could I possibly let it go? So, the only sensible thing to do was to list it for a ridiculous price. That way it would never sell, and my partner would stop nagging at me for buying it in the first place. I think I first relisted it on eBay for £10,000, and it was lucky I wasn't a member of any of the Spice Girls' groups or forums at the time as the 'person' selling the costume online for such a ridiculous amount was absolutely slated. I don't know if I would have been able to recover from that with the fans if they knew it was me that had listed it. My first apology of the book is to the other fans and collectors, I am sorry, I was chancing my arm and £10,000 would have changed our lives at the time and more importantly, secretly it was a ploy to stop my husband moaning at me. I never wanted to sell the costume.

Before owning the costume pieces, I had collected hundreds if not thousands of items of memorabilia. We lived in a modest one-bedroom house in Elderslie (the hometown of William Wallace) in Scotland. The bedroom was full from floor to ceiling with Spice Girls' memorabilia. There was a full Ikea-style bookcase that was overflowing with CDs, vinyls, dolls, Spice Girls' t-shirts, bean bags and teddy bears. The attic was also overflowing with items and every time we opened the hatch something else would fall out on top of us. The whole house was full from top to bottom and every day new packets would arrive containing something else branded with the Spice Girls' faces. Living in Elderslie is where the obsession with collecting was most out of control. There were days when a post van would turn up outside and the postman would make two or three trips to the van for all the boxes and packages specifically for me.

We moved to Cyprus in 2012 to live on a British Military base and I worked at a local military school on the base there. We were posted to Cyprus with Steven's job and what was meant to be an initial 2-year posting turned into 6 amazing years in the glorious sunshine. With that lifestyle though comes some sacrifices and about two weeks after we arrived one of my best friends, Christine suffered a stroke. The first thing I wanted to do was jump on a plane back, but circumstances didn't allow, and I had to sit by the phone and wait for news and updates. You also miss out on other things – gigs, concerts and shows were something that my partner Steven and I used to enjoy a lot. So many live gigs we had to miss out on but strangely the last gig we went to before we moved to Cyprus was Melanie C 'The Sea' tour in Liverpool and it seems it was a bit of an omen as the next place we would move to after Cyprus would be Liverpool, also the next concert I would go to would be Melanie C launching her new album 'Version of Me' at Under the Tunnel in London 6 years later. There was, however, one show we travelled back from Cyprus for, but more about that later...

Living in Cyprus I was missing the collection and I was adding so many items to it but having them delivered to my amazing father-in-law's house in Glasgow. It was only when I would go back for a short holiday to see my friends and family that I would get to see it all. I had to wait almost a year to see all the items I bought from Victoria Beckham's Outnet sale for mothers2mothers (an Aids Charity).

When I did go back to Scotland, it was like Christmas, better than Christmas, better than Birthdays, better than sex, well not quite, but it was a lot of fun. I would sit in the room, open all of the boxes and then put all of the new items in a neat little bundle, much like a five-year-old on Christmas morning.

It was after a trip back to Glasgow and seeing the amount of new costume items that I had amassed that I decided I had to have an exhibition. I'd had the idea before, but this really cemented it for me. How I was going to make that happen I had no idea, but the seed slowly started to grow, and the planning started there. I've never really stopped planning since.

People often ask what my family and partner say about the collection. The truth is, it has involved a lot of arguments, major arguments, I'm leaving you, we're finished kind of arguments. It must be incredibly hard to live with me, or indeed with anyone who is obsessive over something. Every single penny we had was spent on Spice Girls' memorabilia and costumes. There were times where Steven would come home from work and I would have to tell him there was absolutely no money in the bank because I had bought Mel C's trousers from Wembley or a set of Spice Girls dolls' from Spain.

Steven is a saint and deserves a medal. Whilst there have been times where he has been close to killing me, he has always been supportive and always encouraged me to follow my dreams. My own family don't understand it and my dad simply doesn't understand the obsession. It's been a lot of negativity and degrading comments: "Are you stupid?"; "it's beyond ridiculous", and those are the ones I chose to recall. My mum loves me and that has never been in question, but again she doesn't really get it. She didn't get it at all, but I think the first time that she started to was when she came to the London exhibition. I had a conversation with her one day recently where I told her how the Spice Girls had influenced me and what they meant to me, I think she understood that side of it from then but not the collection, not the spending on dolls and stickers and motorbikes and everything else that you could possibly imagine with Spice Girls all over it.

You see, to understand my or indeed anybody's obsession to collect one specific subject then you really need to know what the influence was, where it came from, why it struck home so much, and of course why you would want to own so much 'stuff'.

Well here you go. The Spice Girls released Wannabe in 1996 when I was 15 years old and the unhappiest I have ever been in my life. Everyone has teenage angst, everyone has hormones going crazy but not everyone allows it to get so dark and there were times where my teenage childhood couldn't have got any darker. Failed suicide attempts, self-loathing, self-harm, lashing out and generally in a constant unhappy state of crisis.

When I look back, it wasn't one thing that made me so unhappy it was a whole collection of things. Home life was tough at times but only really in context. We lived in a nice house in a nice area and I went to a nice school, I felt safe most of the time, there was love, there were arguments that got a bit extreme at times and my dad worked a way a lot, but I never really wanted for much.

Mum and dad have been together over 40 years, they were childhood sweethearts and in comparison with today, were still only kids when they got married and fell pregnant. They were young parents and they learned as they were going along.

It wasn't always perfect, far from it. The thing is 40 years later they are still together, and I look at that with pride. As an adult I realise how much they stuck together no matter what.

The Spice Girls were escapism for me, not just that, they were a role model for me. In a time where I was so uncomfortable with myself, with my fat body (seriously fat kid alert), with my sexuality, with home life, with a hundred and one other things.... I lived in a town in Scotland where there was not one openly gay person, I had no real relatable role models, it felt like I was a freak.

These girls launched into an instantly catchy cheesy pop song that I couldn't get enough of and once I got a little bit tired of listening to Wannabe on constant repeat, I turned my attention to the B-side Bumper to Bumper, which was equally catchy and edgy....

> "I beep my horn for you, 'BUMPER TO BUMPER'."

Two songs and I was in love! These girls were amazing, full of attitude, full of fun and with an empowering message of just be yourself.

Girl Power didn't hit home for me in the same way as it did for young girls, but it did hit home. I wanted my mum to be stronger, I wanted the females around me including my girlfriend (yep I had a girlfriend)

Tracey, to be treated more as equals, for them to get a fair crack of the whip. Tracey was strong, fierce and able to take on the world, I honestly think the only reason she didn't like the Spice Girls was because she already had more than enough Girl Power. To Tracey, if you ever read this, I still love you darling, if I wasn't gay, I'd have been happy to spend my life with you and I think about you often.

What got me with the girls was the tongue in cheek, in your face, confident attitude. The whole 'we are taking over and we don't care if you don't like it you are still going to listen to us' attitude. I was instantly addicted to these five young girls who continually told me it was ok to be different, to be individual like them, to have my own character, not to follow like a sheep, and that in general everything would be okay. It was like a reassuring hug through pop music and positivity.

The whole 'work hard and try hard and you can achieve anything' slogan kicked off a spark in me. That frightened, fat, closeted, 15-year-old me would still struggle for another year or so but this is when I started to change. To make decisions to try to escape the life I was in.

I moved away from home at 16 years old, a bit further up north in Scotland to a town called Pitlochry. I was a chef and thought it was the perfect way to get away. To get away from arguments at home which always felt like they were about me. Of course, it wasn't as easy as I thought it would be and

I moved back home a few months later. In fact, I moved back home on 31st August 1997, the day Princess Diana died.

I wasn't back at home for long before I had to get out of there again. It was suffocating, I wanted an adventure and before long I was self-harming again.

After a little trip to the Job centre and a quick phone call I was offered a job in Ireland. I decided it was perfect and off I went at 18 years old to start my own new life in Tralee in Ireland. It was going to be amazing a real adventure, a new start, loads of fun, sex, alcohol and everything else an 18-year-old in the 90s got up to (that's a different book).

I would NEVER have done either of these things if it hadn't been for the Spice Girls making me believe in myself. Making me believe that I deserved better, that I could achieve anything I wanted to, that all you need is positivity and friendship. Friendship Never Ends, well true friendship never ends.

Life began for me after Ireland. I changed. I was a different person. I'd seen life. I'd been through some absolutely horrendous situations on my own. But I felt stronger and more determined for it. I was also a lot more confident and experienced sexually. The years to follow were fun...

It wasn't just that the Spice Girls were around for my angst years but as I started to grow up a little, 19, 20, 21 they were still around and a massive part of pop culture as solo artists. I went to see Melanie C in concert so many times I lost count. I bought all the singles, all the versions if I had the money, and I would buy little bits in the shops if I saw them. The Asda tie, the handkerchiefs, never the dolls as why would a 19-year-old guy in the 90s be buying Spice Girls' dolls. I wasn't allowed, even my friends would have questioned it and so it became almost a secret guilty pleasure.

I'd collect things secretly and stash them in a box. Not massive things but the CDs, DVDs and anything else I could. Of course, one box of items became two and two boxes became three...

They influenced my health and fitness and the decisions I made. I would work out to fitness DVDs trying to get abs like Mel B's, trying to be a better me, because I could, because the Spice Girls told me I could do anything. They literally influenced every part of my life.

By the time Geri released Geri Yoga in 2001 (20 years old) I was down from 16 stone to 11 stone, working out hard and eating very little. Geri yoga helped me slim down my shape even more and it wasn't long until I was just 10 stone and looking a bit worse for it. It seems that belief in yourself wasn't the only thing I learned from Geri as I began controlling food and working out too much.

To take a bit of a leap forward, after a series of disastrous gay relationships (again for another book) I finally met my Steven when I was 23 years old. Just a young baby when I look back. I wasn't sure of him at first and he had to work hard to gain my affection. He was a different kind of quirky and unlike the other clowns I'd dated. I've never looked back and from the day I met him, Steven truly changed my life and made it a better place to be. He literally scraped me off the ground and helped put me back together again. I was homeless a month after meeting him, God knows why he hung around. I must have come across as some kind of mad man that he had just met. Homeless, and literally nothing to my name.

I stayed with Steven for a couple of days on a blow-up mattress and then I stayed with my friend Scott for a couple of months, (on the same blow up mattress) before I managed to secure a flat of my own from the council. It was a horrific time in my life where I had to go and beg for help in a homeless unit. If it wasn't for Steven helping me, I would never have got back on my feet.

He moved in with me a year later, the flat that he had help me to decorate and furnish then became our first home together. It was a one-bedroom tiny council flat in the worst street in the area and everything had to be tied down, but other than that we loved it.

He took me on holiday, he treated me to nights out and we generally had, and still do have, the best time in each other's company. He can make me laugh but also knows exactly when to tell me to stop being a twat.

Most of all, Steven supported me and encouraged me to do well, reaffirmed that I could achieve anything, and here's the impressive bit, he maybe didn't understand it, but he supported me in my collection.

Yes, we had arguments every single time I bought something expensive and yes it put a real strain on our lives at times, but he got it. He understands what they meant to me and how they influenced me, but he also understands the want and need to try and add to the collection. That really, it's an alternative form of savings account and that the possibility of an exhibition of some kind was a real possibility.

I wish we had known that chasing the exhibition and my dream would ultimately be the thing that lead to me losing my beloved Spice Girls' collection. That all the rare one-off costumes, the dolls, the vinyl records and everything else would all have to be sold off and go to new homes in a bid to avoid personal bankruptcy and ending up homeless for a second time in my life.

2

#SpiceUpCyprus

Moving to Cyprus was one of the best decisions of our lives. It shouldn't have been a tough decision but there was a lot to consider. Steven's mum had not long passed away when the job opportunity came up for him and to just up sticks and move everything to another country is a big lifestyle choice. For me it has always been easy to move around and go on the next adventure. I've always been a bit of a gypsy nomad so travelling is a thrill.

We were worried about leaving his dad so soon but as he always does, he encouraged us to go and follow our dreams, not only that but he done everything he could to help us. My father-in-law is a saint, a patient, calm, polite gentleman who believes in and practices positive mentality.

We moved to live on a British military base in Cyprus and to be honest it was an absolute hoot. Steven had a good job, the sun was shining, and we made some amazing friends for life.

I worked part-time in a primary school on the base, working as a classroom assistant and then later as an Emotional Learning Support Assistant. After three years I decided to leave and start up my own business running children's parties, event planning, a party shop and singing. It really was a great but busy little lifestyle.

Moving to a military base there were anxieties; we were unsure how two gay guys living on a military base would get on. We'd never been part of that world before and it was the unknown that was more worrying than anything. However, that was quickly laid to rest as from the moment we got to base everyone was so welcoming. We lived on that base for 6 years by the time we moved back to the UK. The military are the best people in the world, and I mean that sincerely. It taught me a lot living on the base as a civilian outsider. Respect is a massive part of life on base and in the military. It is a small tight knit community and as long as you contribute positively you are welcomed with open arms as one of them.

It also educated me to the importance of the military and the importance of supporting them and their families. They sacrifice a lot whether fighting wars or not and I will forever support military families in any way I can. There were free tickets for troops for the exhibition in all venues in the UK, but I don't think we managed to get it out there enough. I truly take my hat off to them.

When we decided to have an exhibition in Cyprus, when we decided that we were going to ship it over and actually create a show from my collection, the real work began. The logistics for Cyprus were a nightmare from start to finish. It was never going to be easy to ship an entire collection from Scotland to the Island of Cyprus, halfway across the world. It wasn't without risk and we probably took more risks with it than we should have. Insurance was quoted at around £3,000 and it was never purchased. If the ship had sank with the container full of Spice Girls memorabilia, it would all have been lost, all that history but also my whole life savings in a container in the middle of the ocean. It made me feel sick thinking of it all sinking to the bottom of the ocean. The alternative though was to leave it all in boxes up an attic with nobody getting to see it and it slowly rotting away unnoticed.

Working with friends is always a little risky and I am sure Big Dave (the man that can, logistics guy) will agree we really didn't always see eye to eye, especially on the return journey. It's also fair to say that neither of us were in the best head space at that time and whilst Big Dave is a bigger drama queen than any gay guy I know, has the memory span of an excitable spaniel and moans on a level unheard of, he has an absolute heart of gold and is a mate for life (love you Diva Dave). The plus side to working with a mate was the daily updates, Dave was amazing at giving me updates of where the ship was and what the shipping weather was like, this helped the anxiety of it all a little.

I had been without my collection for around three

years by the time it arrived in Cyprus and some of the items I had never seen before. There were new costumes that had arrived that I had never had a chance to see before they were shipped. When it did arrive in Cyprus it took up a large part of our, not small, four-bedroom house and we were tripping over boxes of boxes. Even still, for me it truly was like Christmas had come early and I was so relieved that it all got there in one piece.

I unpacked the boxes like a 4-year-old child that had been eagerly awaiting Santa Claus. I couldn't unwrap it quickly enough and with Steven laughing at my child-like excitement I did what any child would do and built myself a fortress. Not just any fortress but a Spice Girls' fortress. Surrounded by boxes of Spice Girls' memorabilia, dolls, award discs and costume pieces, I was in my 15-year-old self's, actual heaven. Spice Girls' Heaven.

It wouldn't be the last time either.

I was running a business in Cyprus called Party Central Cyprus at this point, so I did have a few business contacts. The venue had been organised through a friend of a friend and it was like that for absolutely everything in Cyprus. It was never about what you know always who you know, who you were friends with and who your friends were friends with or related to. It's a pretty small island and one wrong move and everyone and their cousins would know about it. It wouldn't be long before I knew that all too well.

It's not like in the UK when you can apply for funding, for grants or even for bank loans. I was a visitor in the country and everything had to be funded either by me personally or by obtaining sponsorship for the exhibition. With absolutely every exhibition we have ran, this has been the crux of making it work. Had we obtained any cash sponsorship for Cyprus the situation would not have been anywhere near as bad as it ended up.

We approached a marketing company, who of course put an amazing package together to try and secure us sponsorship (not guaranteed), PR and help us develop the exhibition story. Everything was working well with them and then they handed us the £30,000 invoice.

Realising that just wasn't feasible we tried our very hardest to conquer a market we knew very little about and to be fair on us we did okay with it. The language barrier didn't help and there were obvious cultural barriers with me mincing up to see company directors.

Starting with the venue it was very clear that Cypriots value everything they are selling you very highly and value everything you are selling them very low. There is normally enough money in their bank account that they would rather have an empty venue than compromise on unreasonable prices. This is also the same with house rentals and many gorgeous villas are left empty rather than compromise with the market.

We looked at a few venues and whilst some of them would have been a lot cheaper for us we found a venue right beside the brand new multi-million-pound Limassol Marina and with a wealth of history it blew us away when we were looking around it.

The first visit to the venue was farcical and wouldn't be out of place in the movie 'My Big Fat Greek Wedding'. Demetris, a photographer that I had worked with had told me that he was 'best friends' with the owner of the venue and that we had an appointment to go and view the venue one Saturday evening.

Demetris insisted on meeting for drinks beforehand and despite the fact that I had asked him on several occasions not to bring his children with him, there he was sitting in the restaurant with three young children, all under 8 years old, one in a buggy, ready to go to this business meeting about a prospective venue for the exhibition.

After Demetris had finished feeding the kids we wandered over to the venue to have a look around. I was asking if we had to go in the back way or to an office when Demetris lead me straight up to the front door, past the security guards waving his hands shouting he was friends with the manager, and marched all five of us, me him and his three kids (one in a buggy), right into the middle of a massive Cypriot society wedding. Grabbing a glass of champagne, Demetris casually started interacting whilst his children swept around the swarms of who's who of Cyprus in some of the most incredible gowns ever.

Unsurprisingly when Demetris eventually tracked down the extremely frantic manager, he knew nothing of the meeting and swiftly asked Demetris what the hell he was doing there. I apologised profusely and asked if possible, to contact him at a later date when he was slightly less busy.

Mortified I dragged Demetris and his three children, including the one in the buggy, out of the building as fast as I could and demanded to know what on earth he was thinking. "Ah Alan, don't worry, this is how we do things in Cyprus". Yeah, whatever buddy, you are a halfwit and I am utterly mortified!

I later gave Demetris another chance to work on the exhibition, but this is really where I quickly learned that as soon as I mentioned to anyone I owned the collection and was having an exhibition, they immediately saw cash signs and attempted to charge as much as they possibly could for anything. He quoted £6,000 to take pictures for the first Cyprus programme and we never really spoke again. There was an angry Facebook post from me which followed, I didn't tag Demetris in it, but since I worked with his wife Moira it did cause some unfriendly ripples, and I learned maybe not to have public rants quite as much? Well... I tried to learn.

It was always lessons learned the hard way for me really. I'm glad we started in Cyprus, it taught me my trade and taught me to walk away from deals that were not quite right. Something, that with a little more experience, I really would have done a lot more of.

Cyprus was much easier than London in other ways. It was completely my exhibition with no other collectors or designers to work around. I had full control over absolutely everything to do with it and I really enjoyed that. The other thing that always makes things easier in Cyprus is less health and safety hoops to jump through, less red tape. This has pluses and negatives I suppose, the pyrotechnics guy we met with three fingers would probably say it was a bad thing, at the same time as holding up a lit indoor firework with his other hand with only four fingers remaining.

It was amazing to start with an idea, a visual in my head and then work hard to turn it into a reality. The design had to change shape a couple of times due to costs of building staging in Cyprus. I'm so glad we didn't go with a round birthday cake style tiered stage, the cost was over 20,000 euros and there is no way I could have afforded to ship it back or store it. Instead we used 1m x 2m segments of staging borrowed from the venue. This is the design we then used in London, the smaller stages can be built up and they're flexible to fit into any space in any venue.

There were so many aspects to the exhibition that were a challenge and of course I done what I always do, and bitten off way more than I could chew.

Unrealistic timelines for production of the book and reading material placed huge strain and pressure on me and I was often up researching and writing material all night. Getting a couple of hours sleep and then working a full day the next day again. It really was burn out material and it wasn't long until it started to have an effect.

Whilst we tried our hardest to keep the costs to a minimum there was the basics that we had to resource and of course if it could not be sourced on the island, it would have to be shipped. Mannequins were our first big hurdle and we needed a lot. I had over 100 pieces of Spice Girls' clothing in the collection at this point, some of them really iconic and some of them just pairs of denims worn on stage. We needed around 60 mannequins, they weren't all full mannequins but off we went to speak to Cypriot shop fitting companies. 400 euros per mannequin, 300 for legs, it was beyond crazy prices. Surely there is no way in the world anyone is paying that for a mannequin? £100 from even an expensive supplier in the UK sees you with a good showcase mannequin, seriously how can anyone justify 400 euros? They should have had balaclavas on!

Shipping 60 mannequins over to Cyprus wasn't easy and of course they would have to be shipped back as well. Not only that but the house was already full of collection. Where the hell were we going to store 60 mannequins? Stacked in my living room for months and months it seems. In any space that we could fit something it was jam-packed in. Having the house absolutely full of boxes is something I have really struggled with. We lived in a gorgeous big house in Cyprus yet it was constantly just a complete tip and overflowing with 'stuff'.

Trying to get sponsors involved in Cyprus was harder than anything else. I had a few business contacts through running my Party Central business and this would help us with the entertainment side of it but again in Cyprus it is not what you know but who you know. When some gay, crazy Spice Girls' collector you have never heard of contacts some 60-year-old head of company who probably still watches a black and white TV and has never heard of the Spice Girls, to invest in my exhibition, to hand over money or products to be involved, this was an impossible task and it would have been more time efficient if we had realised this from the start.

It was the same situation with the Cyprus PR company. There isn't really such a thing as a Cypriot PR company that covers arts and exhibitions, the island is too small. What you do have is a couple of guys here and there that run a sports PR company with lots of lad contacts but not much else. This coupled with the laid-back sunshine attitude, and no VIP guests had even been invited two weeks before the launch. Nightmare.

Cultural differences and a slight language barrier definitely played a part in putting barriers in place and everything that should have been a relatively simple task took three times as long as it should have.

Nothing quite prepared us for the build week though......

Without doubt one of the most physically demanding weeks of my life and I can't thank the people involved enough for their help.

The temperature outside was 42 degrees but inside we had no air conditioning (it wasn't allowed on during build days due to cost) the stage lighting was being tested and there were bodies everywhere building staging, building mannequins, putting together sign posts. At one point it was well over 50 degrees in the main hall. We couldn't even open a door for a breeze as the moment we did people started wandering in to see what was going on. Cypriots are naturally inquisitive.

Steven and I were at the venue every day of the build, he had arranged time off, so it was very early morning starts and late-night finishing, but in the middle of July in Cyprus even at 7am it is 30 degrees, there is literally no let up. The one plus side was that we each lost about a stone and a half in weight in a week.

I don't know if nerves and stress made it worse, but I was vomiting every day at this point. I had stomach ulcers from a medication I had taken for years and it made me unable to eat, unable to keep anything down and I would throw up on a very regular basis.

If I was too hot, if I was too cold, if I was worried, if I drank alcohol. Absolutely everything made me throw up and the build week of the exhibition was no different. The launch night was worse. It felt like I was throwing up every five minutes, every time I moved, I felt queasy and would inevitably have to run to the toilet to throw up or at least wretch for five minutes.

Friends were coming to help us, but it really was a hard slog and we couldn't expect anything more than an hour or two in the heat. People would end up exhausted and ready to jump in a swimming pool and we would have to plough on to try and get it finished. Sometimes jumping in the pool when we got home at 9 or 10pm.

Despite all the moaning I am doing, #SpiceUpCyprus was an absolute buzz at this point. All the years and months of work were really starting to take shape and it was looking better than I ever could have imagined. There was always a doubt, do I have enough for an exhibition, will it look enough, have I laid it out and designed it well, millions and millions of questions of self-doubt.

There was one point when the stages were in, the mannequins were built, the lighting was in place, the timeline was hanging from the wall and all that was left to do was dress the exhibition. The moment I look around at other people's faces and see the light bulb moment of 'wow this is huge'. I still didn't believe I could fill it even though in my head I knew exactly where every single thing was going to go, right down to the CDs and movie stickers.

Technical duties have never been my strong point, so other than maybe hooking up some lighting, the technical side such as sound, projectors or anything else that needs hooking up and a laptop, it's over to Steven. I need to add that Steven hates this. He can do it and he always figures out how it works but, I am not allowed to talk to him during the process and most of the time it is best to stay out the way and let him argue with the equipment, kick it and eventually be delighted that's it's working. Steven loves nothing more than making me happy, and when things are working I am happy, so he tries to fix everything, he's awesome.

Being drenched in sweat is not the nicest feeling but not only that it is really hard to get enough liquids into you when you are constantly dripping with sweat and throwing up. I was on all sorts of medication just to try and keep going. Anti-sickness tablets, rehydration sachets, plus all my usual medication for my thyroid and other old man ailments. It's a wonder I didn't rattle when I walked. Along with the schedule comes no time to get anything else sorted, no nutritious meals, or anything of substance. We were surviving on protein bars, ice-cream and bottles and bottles of water but of course as soon as it was in my stomach it was straight back out.

The other issue with sweating so much is that it goes

everywhere. The minute you touch a plastic mannequin it immediately has a sweaty imprint on it and of course despite the fact they have on stage, you can't sweat all over the Spice Girls' stage costumes or indeed the memorabilia. So, the next issue was having to wipe anything and everything that had marks on it, marks that showed up 100 times more with the stage lighting on them.

Steven doesn't ask for much and doesn't put his foot down very often, so when he does, I tend to give in and let him have what it is that he wants. My mistake here was asking him and letting him have the thought because when I asked him what he wanted to wear for the red-carpet launch evening he of course being a proud Scotsman insisted on a kilt. 40-degree heat and Steven wants to wear a fucking kilt, kill me now......

I've mentioned it above but part of my thyroid condition is that I tend to sweat a lot, so when it is hot I sweat a lot more and then when you add heavy tartan, a jacket and bow tie on top of that, I was literally like the wicked witch of the west, melting.

Getting the exhibition to a stage where it was ready to open to the public was one of if not the hardest and most stressful things I have ever had to do (well apart from when we did it in London again) and it broke me physically.

On the day of the launch it was the finishing touches and we had a great little team of people around us helping us out. Against the odds we managed to pull together the technical side, the exhibition was looking amazing, the VIP gift bags were sorted, the red carpet was out, and I had to trust the PR company, the catering company and everyone else, were ready to go. It was time to go home and get ourselves ready to launch my first ever exhibition: #SpiceUpCyprus.

I was so nervous about the launch evening, more nervous than I had ever been about anything in my life. Getting married was nerve wracking but to be honest I was so hungover the day we got married the first time, that I was just relieved to get through the day. This was different, this was something I had worked on for years, something I had looked forward to and dreamt of since the day I got my hands on that Pepsi costume. I'd seen it all set up with all the lights, projections and sound running, it was incredible, and I was so happy with how it looked but that didn't stop me being nervous.

Everything was so rushed that it blurs, and I really have to sit and think about it to work out the events and how it all happened. It helps chatting to Steven, Mr Rain Man remembers every detail about everything.

We had arranged some amazing entertainment for the evening and had invited everyone from the head of the Military in Cyprus to the President of the Country. We knew it was ambitious but given that we had been involved in entertainment across the country we were hopeful a few of our contacts would turn up to support us.

Driving home from the venue was about a half hour drive and there was a limo booked to pick us up around 6.30pm for a 7pm(ish) arrival. On the way home Steven had to stop the car for me to be sick and then, when I was in the shower trying to cool down, I was sick again. It wasn't a great start and I'd already taken all the medication I could.

Putting on the kilt and trying to get ourselves ready in the heat was harsh, I was trying my hardest to get to the venue without my shirt being soaked through and without being sick another twenty times.

The Limo arrived at the house and my stomach flipped again, not throwing up luckily but for the first time I'd realised it was really happening. It was built, all the arrangements were made and in place for the launch evening. I was so happy with how the exhibition looked all set out in the venue and with everything including the tech on it, it was spectacular. Being happy with the result didn't stop me from being nervous as hell, I have performed on stage in front of thousands of people, but this was my heart and soul, laid out for everyone to have an opinion of. This was years of hard work and sacrifices, it was never bought with the sole intention of showcasing it but now that I was doing exactly that, I was more nervous than I'd ever been in my life.

Steven and I got into the limo and immediately asked for the aircon to be blasting at us, the kilts were so heavy and hot, but I couldn't help but stop for a second and notice how handsome my husband was and how happy he was with what we were doing. He was proud of what we had worked hard to achieve, he doesn't need to say it, you can see it.

We picked up two of my best friends on the way there, driving through Cyprus in a limo is a strange experience, not only does everyone look but the roads aren't really designed for them and it's a bit of a bumpy ride at times.

As we turned around the corner in Kolossi (a tiny little village in Cyprus) we could see Nand and Bonnie standing at the side of the road waiting for the limo to turn up. They both looked so stunning and glamorous and I am beyond grateful that they were there to keep me calm. I don't have a clue what was said in the car, I just remember sitting trying not to sweat, trying not to throw up and trying not to pass out with nervousness.

Pulling up outside the venue in Cyprus was a bit of a crazy moment for us. It was Steven who had said let's turn up in style with the kilts and the limo, it was a nice finishing touch but I was a bit shocked when we got there and a couple of press photographers ran up to the car and starting taking pictures before the door had even opened. A little bit dazed by the flashbulb I tried my very best to smile and give my best peace sign. I'm sure most of the pictures were sent to a comedy sketch show.

It was beyond gorgeous and everything I had imagined it to be. Like a proper London style movie premier, the red carpet was gorgeous and lined by 4ft high light up letters spelling out Girl Power of course. There was a massive scaffolding square with search lights searching the sky, Spice Girls' music blaring and a sleek logo press board.

Wearing the kilts was a stroke of genius in the middle of Cyprus, even if I was melting like the wicked witch, it had done the job with the press and before long I was whisked inside to carry out press interview after press interview. It was my first ever experience of it and whilst I was incredibly nervous, I tried my best to put my confident head and face on, face the cameras and gush about these amazing ladies who changed my life. Hardly a task.

I don't have any real memory of the interviews and I couldn't tell you one question that I was asked but I do know I spent most of the time I was talking trying my hardest not to throw up. Purposefully swallowing the saliva in my mouth so that I was concentrating on something rather than hurling.

After seeing me running to the toilet for about the tenth time, grandad (my bestie Stevie C) came and said enough is enough, you need to stop and let's go outside for a smoke.

What he meant by that is that he had a joint in his pocket and that it would help calm me down and hopefully stop my me throwing up so violently. He was right as always. I took one draw of it and threw up everywhere, after that we smoked the rest of it, and I wasn't sick for hours. I don't know whether it was just enough to calm me down or whether it genuinely helped my stomach but from that moment on I was able to return inside and have a great time with all the guests. Medical Marijuana is something that is starting to appear in British society, but I strongly believe the benefits of this for many ailments needs to be researched and shared with open minds.

We'd arranged the entertainment for the whole evening, a 50-strong ladies choir made up of military wives and British expats in Cyprus, Kirsty Dewar, and an amazing band called Coindrop.

The choir was made up of some real friends from Cyprus including Clare (Bonkers) West who was one of my most trusted buddies. It was hard to keep it together emotionally as I stood amongst friends and family and watched this powerhouse group of females belt out some of my most cherished Spice Girls' songs. Mama, Viva Forever and Goodbye all sound amazing when sung by a choir. The ladies really did us proud and it was one of the moments in life when everything seems a bit surreal. Surrounded by our nearest and dearest in Cyprus listening to some more of our nearest and dearest sing some of my favourite songs. Wow just wow ladies, thank you so much for this!

As Kirsty took to the stage after the choir the tempo of the night started to increase and by the time Coindrop came on we were in full blown party mode. All the acts sang Spice Girls and whilst it was a really nice touch it wasn't overpowering in any way.

The turnout of local celebs and characters could have been better so much so that the PR company apologised for letting us down with the guestlist and removed the charges for this off the bill. Nice touch to remove the charges but it didn't change the fact the place should have been full of the who's who of Cyprus. In another way it was lucky as with the rabble of our nearest and dearest drinking all the champagne and Spice Girls' themed cocktails, the bar ran out of half of the drinks about an hour before the end.

The whole experience is a total blur and other people remember bits of it that I don't. I think that is the same with most of life's big events, but I have definitely lost my recollection of this through the adrenaline.

By chance my cousin was in Cyprus on holiday with her family, none of the rest of my family had flown over to see the exhibition, but it was genuinely lovely to have my big cousin Gilian there with her husband and daughter. I didn't get anywhere near enough time with them as I would have hoped, and they were meant to be coming in a limo with a Geri drag queen, but she cancelled on us last minute.

I remember, later on in the evening when the band were rocking out to one of our favourite songs, Steven and I were bouncing around wild with our kilts on, unfortunately I think maybe I'd lost a little bit too much weight during the building process and I very nearly lost the kilt completely. It was only with a last second grab that I managed to stop it from falling down completely.

It wasn't long until the launch evening was all over, and although we perhaps didn't have the numbers we would have liked, it was a massive success and I am so proud that we managed to pull it off in such style. There was enough VIP attendance that it made the Cyprus news, so I guess we caused enough of a fuss that night at least.

It has been said that I am one of the most unorganised people in the world but here I was not only arranging and building an exhibition in a different country, but I was pulling off an event of this size and scale. It was slick, impressive and ran just the way I had wanted it to. The red carpet, the exhibition, the entertainment, the guests, the cocktails, the food….. everything was slick and smooth.

The next morning wasn't so slick and smooth when we had to try and get ourselves together to go and open the exhibition and run it for a solid 8 hours.

Driving to the venue hungover, the hangover for one of the only times ever in my life was almost irrelevant. We had a job to do and an exhibition to get ready for the public. There was no time to be hungover, we both had to pull on our big boy pants and get on with it.

Pre-ticket sales in Cyprus were not great but we always expected that as Cyprus isn't the most technologically advanced country, no food apps or anything like that. We were going for local tourist trade, the expat community, Russians and of course Cypriots. The problem was, tapping into these markets, as we found, was nearly impossible and despite our best efforts, well, we didn't quite get there with it. The biggest problem with tapping into these markets is that they all use different social media platforms, the Russians have their own version of Facebook that they use, and the Cypriots, that was a hard market to crack with anything.

Saturday 23rd July 2016 is the day we opened the doors to my first ever Spice Girls' exhibition. The Trakasol Cultural Centre in Limassol Cyprus is a stunning venue with lots of cultural history to offer as well. It was built in the early 1900s and as it was situated close to the old port of Limassol it was perfect for storing items being shipped out of Cyprus, namely Carobs, one of Cyprus' biggest exports.

We'd worked our asses off, given blood, sweat and tears and created an amazing tribute to five incredible ladies that meant the world to me. The only problem is, nobody else in Cyprus really cared, and if they did care they couldn't be bothered to give up valuable holiday beach time to walk about in an indoor exhibition. If we had managed to attract enough sponsorship to offer it as a free exhibition then it would have been a bit of a different story and loads of people would have enjoyed it.

There is always a nice story to tell, the first person through the door though was a delight. A little Girl called Libby that had come down with her mum as she loved the Spice Girls. She danced her way up to the desk announced that she had been listening to Spice Girls all the way there and she couldn't wait to see the exhibition. I think Libby was five at the time if I remember rightly and she spent the whole time spinning around in circles and dancing around the exhibition. One of the things that is special about running an event or an exhibition is getting to see people enjoying themselves, carefree and dancing around at something you have worked so hard to create.

The only problem with the exhibition, was at the price we were paying for the venue and the running costs, the 30 visitors a day were nowhere near enough to sustain it, not only that but we were losing money hand over fist.

When you're starting a business or a concept from scratch in a foreign country, there is no government funding available, no business grants, short term loans or indeed anything else. By the time the exhibition opened its doors in Cyprus we had ploughed a massive £40,000 into it, a mixture between our own money and money mostly borrowed from my father-in-law.

All of this was done because we were so sure that it would work, so sure that we were able to create something special (which we did), so sure that we would get the numbers. We had never for one second contemplated that we wouldn't get the people through the door, so sitting there with one or two people every half an hour was soul destroying. It was literally like we could see all the hopes of it working draining away. Our dreams of taking it on tour and making it our working business were getting further and further away from us.

It got to a stage where we had to close the exhibition early and not lose any more money. It was beyond devastating and suddenly, we realised that we had lost everything we had ever worked towards. Not only had we ploughed everything we had into the exhibition we were now in over £40,000 worth of debt, and it was catastrophic to us.

We have become good at putting a brave face on now but at that time it was a whole new ball game for us, and it was hard to grin and bear it, but we did. With smiles on our faces we welcomed our last few guests to the exhibition and closed after a run of two weeks. Looking back and writing this book I am so proud of what we achieved as a team. There simply wasn't the audience we needed, and it was 100 percent in the wrong country.

Pulling the exhibition apart was painful, we were broke, our spirits were broken, we were physically broken with heat exhaustion and I really don't know how we did it.

I do know that once it was done, we didn't dare talk about the Spice Girls for at least two weeks after it. We spent some time in the pool trying to heal ourselves and taking any time that we could to just stew. Stew in our own thoughts, stew in the chat, stew in the misery that we owed so much money, panic that we owed so much money and try against all odds to get ourselves back to some kind of normality. I don't know how we did it or when we started doing it but slowly, very slowly we started to dig out of the hole a little bit more each day.

3

Picking Ourselves Up Off The Floor

It wasn't easy to pick ourselves up off the floor and the aftermath of Cyprus was horrendous! Our whole world seemed to fall apart and on top of the realisation that the exhibition had failed to set the world on fire, we now had people chasing us on an hourly basis for money. The venue for one though were different, happy with the payments we made and in the knowledge we had tried our hardest. When we went scouting for the venues in Cyprus the original price they wanted to charge us for Trakasol Cultural Centre was 3,000E per day. I wish I had been a little more experienced in this area, it seemed an awful lot of money and to cover costs of the venue alone we would need 300 people through the door, that's ok though as we were going to get thousands, so we thought. There are venues in Central London that wouldn't charge you 3000E per day. One thing I will give Cypriots is they know their worth, they maybe think too much of it at times and unlike Brits they are unwilling to negotiate for the best part. Either you take their deal, or they would rather have the venue empty and being unused. Luckily the Trakasol were not like that and we did manage to negotiate and get the price down by at least half I am sure.

The caterers were chasing for the final payment due to them, the lighting company were chasing for the payments due to them, but luckily and unlike London, that was really everything that we could get on a pay later basis in Cyprus, unfortunately all the money we had ploughed in was now lost but we could start just ever so slightly to see that there could maybe be a way out. A way that we could pay everyone and move on with life.

We turned our attention to the shop and my Party Central business and before long we were working 80-hour weeks just to try and pay off some of the money that had been promised out. Grandad had helped us out (Stevie C) and so he had to get the money back we owed him as well. We sold off our pride and joy 'Jeff the Jeep' and sold off our second car.

We did it though. We paid the caterers, we paid grandad, we paid the lighting company (well 90% of a ridiculous bill anyway) and with the exception of my father-in-law, who we still owed an absolute fortune to, most non- family members were paid.

We had had the wind well and truly knocked out of our sails and we had no idea how the hell we were going make it through the challenges ahead. Together as always.

We never once put it out online that the exhibition

hadn't really worked out that well for us. Instinctively I wanted to protect what we had achieved. I knew we had the mannequins, the first run of the book, all the showcasing materials and aids and we also knew how amazing it looked. People who had been to the exhibition loved it, loved the vibe and spent hours in it.

Before long, a little niggling thought started creeping in with us all. By us all I mean Steven, Grandad, Nand, Me, and Alex my designer, who later became my amazing PA.

Grandad was convinced it would work in London and with his usual charm, excitement and enthusiasm it wasn't long until Stevie C had us all thinking that London was the place to go.

'You should have a permanent museum dedicated to them in London' was easily his favourite suggestion and Stevie C is not one for letting it go once he gets something in his head.

After #SpiceUpCyprus it was hard to even contemplate putting ourselves through that ever again. The trouble is we really believed in it. We'd got it wrong with Cyprus, it wasn't the right place for us, it was the wrong time of year, the exact location was wrong within the newly built marina, and we had overestimated the Cypriot interest. I later found out that during the 90s most people in Cyprus still had black and white TVs and TV was not a part of cultural life. Basically, most of the Cypriots had no idea who the Spice Girls were or if they did, they had even less inkling to go to an exhibition about them.

What Cyprus did allow us to do was see how it looked when it was showcased and lit properly. To see that we could curate it and organise it so that it looked amazing. An aesthetically pleasing but informative experience as well. Anyone that did come to it, absolutely loved it.

London was always the place that it was destined for. People were telling me all the time that we needed to go to London. Stevie C was constantly becoming animated when chatting about London.

> "Fucking hell mate, can you imagine the amount of people that will come see it in London? You need to set up a permanent museum for them in central London, everyone will come see it."

Do you know what, he is right. I still believe now that if we set it up somewhere permanent it would become a top attraction a bit like the Beatles museum in Liverpool. There were loads of people that came straight to the exhibition in Angel from the Eurostar. We had an article in the Eurostar magazine and they were reading it on the journey and turning up with their suitcases. It was beyond amazing.

It was difficult at the time though to see how we would ever be able to afford another exhibition. Even though we had most of the display aids we needed, we still had to get them back to the UK, we still had to get the collection back and we still had to get ourselves back. One big stumbling block was that we had no real timescale for moving.

Throughout the exhibition and even in the aftermath of Cyprus I had been keeping in contact with some of the other collectors. Liz West and I were messaging backwards and forwards on Facebook and it was just after this I think that we started talking properly on Skype.

It was strange at first talking to another collector, but at the same time instantly you have something pretty unique in common. We could talk for hours about the Spice Girls and we did on a few occasions. We chatted about costume pieces we both had and where they had come from. Liz and I have built a friendship since. It's a strange friendship. Both of us are very different with the exception of a huge passion for the Spice Girls and there have been times over the past two years where we have been raging at each other. That's another strange thing about our friendship. Even though we are still getting to know each other in the grand scheme of life, having only really chatted for a few years, we can have a screaming raging argument with each other over something and tell each other to fuck right off. But then half an hour later we will send a little text, it won't be an apology text, it will be an olive branch with no kisses at the end of it and then of course before long we are chatting like normal again.

Getting to know Liz is hard as she doesn't trust

easily, but over time, I think we got there mostly.

One of the deciding factors for having the London exhibition was new costumes that I had secured through talking with Liz. Liz had been offered a job lot of costumes from the Istanbul tour producer. She had bought them all, struck a deal and then made a separate deal to sell some of the outfits on to me. I'm not sure what Liz paid for it all. I've never asked and don't really care to be honest. I was just delighted that the items had surfaced and were no longer being kept locked away in a cupboard or under a bed.

I bought the silver space suits from the Spice Girls Move Over performance in their first ever live concert in Istanbul. Stunning metallic reflective material that was made into space suit style all-in-ones, well apart from Victoria's which of course is a mini dress version. I remember watching the concert scene where the girls wore these on stage, over and over again when I was younger. At the end of performing Move Over and after writhing around on the stage floor, the girls ripped the spacesuits off to reveal other costumes underneath them, a truly magical stage moment that I still watch and smile at now.

Another set of costumes that I bought from Liz at this time, was the full line up of 'Naked' robes. Massive black robes with hoods on them, they are very imposing on display and unlike anything else the Spice Girls wore on stage. These are huge robes and one of the only costumes I have ever been able to try on. The girls wore the robes onto stage, sat on chairs that were positioned back to front, hid their bodies behind the chairs and dropped the robes to the floor to sing the song. The Spice Girls were naked to sing Naked, get it? It worked well as an illusion on stage but of course they were never fully naked. Geri's corset and Mel B's boob tube were also items bought in that same lot from Liz.

Of course, money was incredibly tight for us at the time, #SpiceUpCyprus had failed, we still owed £40,000 at this point and here I am making a deal with Liz for a five figure sum to buy even more Spice Girls' stage costumes. Steven was beyond furious with me and was continually telling me to tell Liz I couldn't buy them. Problem with that is that by this point I have already got my heart set on owning them and putting them into my next exhibition. Even at this point I wouldn't give up. I was starting to believe that maybe it could be done and maybe London was the place to take it.

Liz was fairly understanding and patient in waiting for payments from us. It suited her as much as us though and I'm positive Liz made the deal work very well for her. Whilst a friend, Liz is also a businesswoman, fierce, why wouldn't she be she is Girl Power personified, however there are ways and means of doing business and ways of speaking to people and we definitely clashed heads a few times over that.

It wasn't easy to dust myself off and get on with it. I

was wounded, my pride was battered, we were skint beyond believe and it always seemed like I was just adding more and more pressure to us financially.

I couldn't rush into anything, but I very slowly started contacting some museums, following venues on social media, building the social media platform again and generally getting back into the swing of it all. Spiceworld is a strange place to be and you need to know the basics and how protective the fans are over the girls. One wrong move and your whole target market are going to take a massive dislike to you. I've seen that happen with other people. I'm sure I am not the most popular person in the world, but Liz has had hate mail and people trolling her online. Thankfully everyone has always been lovely to me and I try to be my usual friendly self with everyone else.

I had started to sell some items off from the collection to try and help pay back some of the money that we owed and to help get us back on our feet. Nothing that was irreplaceable, I had some doubles of dancers' costumes and a few extra bits and pieces, which helped a little.

The conversations with other Spice Girls' collectors were growing. If I was going to do this again and it was a big "IF", then I wanted it to be even bigger and better than what we had created in Cyprus. The other collectors were really open to being involved although some needed a little more time than others to jump on the band wagon.

It was a passion project from start to finish and with the other collectors: Andrea; Samuel; Liz; Jyle; and of course, the lovely David, it was also their passion! With a loan of their items I was positive I could create something that was out of this world fantastic and a fitting tribute to the world's biggest ever girl band.

Now all I needed was a plan of action and some money, even a tenner would have been nice!

4

Sprouting Routes

Once Liz was paid off for the costumes, I started really turning my attention to London. With Nand, Stevie C and my Steven all now thinking it could work I was starting to get excited about the prospect of a London exhibition. This time it would have to be bigger and better.

I started researching venues first, without a venue in place there was no point in even trying to look at anything else. I didn't know London well at the time and there is no way in the world I could have found my way around it on my own. My geographical knowledge was shocking so venues were looked at on suitability, the rest could be whittled down. I was looking at whether they were central London, East London or anywhere else, the initial list was made purely on suitability.

Venues are crazy, they have to sell themselves and they have to try and get the best price they can for the venue but to try and charge £20,000 per day for a venue hire is beyond crazy, even in London. I can honestly say that none of the venues we are viewed were ever worth that amount of money and I was obviously wrong in my previous thinking of hire costs.

It took me weeks and weeks to try and compile a list of possible venues from the internet. It's not easy and you have to wade through every venue agency there is. It's seems that venues don't really advertise themselves anymore but do it through some venue finder app or website. That combined with my complete lack of geographical knowledge of London we ended up with a list of around 20 different venues dotted from one end of London to the other.

Twenty venues, each of them unique and different in their own way, was at least a good starting point and now the exhibition in London was no longer a pipe dream but something I've researched and spent a lot of time on already by this point. If you have ever worked on a project the more you work on it the more passionate about it you become and the more determined you become to make it happen.

By July 2017, only 12 months after the Cyprus exhibition, it was time to head to London and have a look at the venue possibilities. Armed with a list of twenty it was going to be nearly impossible to get it down to one, or so we thought. In reality, 20 became 11 within a couple of hours of working out accurate locations and geography. We were able to score a few off before we went to see them, purely on the distance from the nearest tube.

I flew from Cyprus to Birmingham and went to stay

at Nand's house in Coventry for the first time. Nand's house is amazing, not only is it all warm and welcoming, everything is pink, and I mean everything! It's called the Pink Palace for a reason, the sofa is pink, the rug is pink, the chairs are pink, the bedding is pink, the toilet roll is pink, everything in the kitchen is pink, the car is pink and in amongst all of this pink there are elephants everywhere. Nand also collected elephants, elephant bedding, elephant statues, elephant pictures, elephant earrings, she even had a very special elephants tattoo.

It's hard to sum Nand up in a way that truly gives you a good picture of her and of her infectiousness. Nand was a drama teacher, she didn't always like kids that much but when they were in drama having fun and letting their hair down her little face would light up. With cropped hair that was always died pink and cropped little legs that kept her at a cool 5 ft 1 or 2 maybe, whilst small in stature her personality more than made up for it. You could never be too serious around Nand because if things took a dark turn she would simply make a face, say something silly, drool on purpose, open her mouth and show you chewed food or something equally as mental.

From Coventry we got the train down to London and that's where the fun really began. It felt like a fun adventure with my best friend, not really like work at all but that's exactly what we were there for. The train itself was a laugh as we played the silliest of association games, taking them to ridiculous levels of rudeness and we loved making plans of our days and what we were going to do beyond the venue scouting.

The hotel was Nand's choice. I'd previously told her about a bad experience I had with Steven booking a hostel for us to stay in once that was full of bugs (my 30th birthday trip to Vegas and Steven booked a hotel close to the airport for about £20, it was great value for money as there were at least 20 pounds worth of bugs!). Nand insisted she knew this lovely hotel called the Grand Royale just beside Hyde park and she wasn't wrong. It was the former home of Lilly Langtry (Google her, very interesting character). It was really central and really grand as the name would suggest.

Nand and I were like giddy school children as we were checking in to the hotel, laughing and giggling whilst talking about pinching the flowers and fake fruit on the front desk. The hotel was irrelevant really, it was the company that was amazing. Nand and I always had great adventures together, putting the world to rights and finding the fun in everything, normally with a glass of wine in hand.

Getting into the room was no different. We opened the door to the room and Nand asked if she could have the bed away from the window and closest to the bathroom. She dumped her bags and launched a full-blown superman leap on to the bed. As she landed the beds split in two and little tiny Nand disappeared in between the two of them, one leg and one arm stuck in the air, I could just see the top of her little pink head bobbing up and down as she silently laughed at first. The silent laughter didn't last for long and we were both buckled on the floor laughing hysterically at how stupid Nand had been. I am laughing writing this! My crazy little friend Nand, what an amazing start we were having to our exciting London adventure.

We weren't able to have much downtime. I had literally arranged for us to be jumping from one venue viewing to the next. We had two and a half days in London and if I didn't have a venue chosen by the end of the trip then not only was the trip fruitless but there was no way timescales would work. There was not enough time to be doing a second site visit. It's not that easy to jump back from Cyprus every week for business meetings, so it was essential we capitalised.

Within 30 mins of getting there we were turned around and back out the hotel heading to our first venue viewing. With a real mixed bag of venues the first one put us on a back foot straight away and it turned out to be easier than we thought to start ruling out venues one by one.

The first we went to view was the building attached to Westminster Abbey. It's a massive building that is all interlocked. It had a huge domed room in it and was very regal. Making our way through the corridors we were in awe of the details in the architecture and the paintings on the roof. It really was a pretty magical place and although we ruled it out as a venue instantly, it really was a privilege to have a tour around this magnificent building. The fact that it was also the operating building of the clergy associated with Westminster Abbey, we thought it best not to ask them if we could blare out Wannabe through the PA system.

Had I been in London with Steven I would have been dragged from pillar to post with my walking shoes worn out within a day. Thankfully Nand (with tiny little legs) was not a massive fan of walking miles, so it was taxis or the tube wherever we went, and I have to say it felt amazing to be scooting around London from one stunning venue to the next on time limited site visits. Not only that but everyone we met was very welcoming and treated us like we were important, I suppose renting a venue for a month is a pretty big deal.

By the end of the first day we were already tired, and even though we were not walking for miles on end, it was rushed, pressured and stressful trying to get around London (especially for a little country boy like me haha). We had managed to rule out four of the five venues that we had viewed on the first day. It was nice to chat through it with Nand and rather than have a really heated passionate debate (like Steven and I would have done) it was sensible pros and cons, can we definitely rule it out style chats.

One of the highlights I have had from organising the whole exhibition was that few days I had in London with Nand. It was magical and although we had been friends for years we had never been away anywhere together. It was full on but also full of fun.

The highlight of that trip to London was undoubtedly the trip to the theatre to see the Meatloaf musical Bat Out of Hell. We had managed to get tickets that day and Nand was so excited about it. I was brought up with my dad listening to and singing Meatloaf constantly, so at least I knew the songs and was with my little pink bestie. It was bloody brilliant from start to finish, the staging was amazing, at one point a full-sized Cadillac went crashing off the stage and into the orchestra pit. The songs were incredible, the plot was maybe a little thin but everything else made up for it and my little pink nelly was almost jumping out her seat with excitement every two minutes. Singing along, gasping in reaction to the set changes and storyline, crying, and dancing her little ass off. Nand and I were in our element, having the time of our lives.

The second day of the trip was absolutely jam-packed with venues to view and I think in total we had 8 to fit in to one day. Nand was a legend at getting us up and organised and out of the hotel on time. From then on, she was in navigation mode. We agreed that I could concentrate on social media updates and posts whilst she would work out the tubes etc. There is no way I could have navigated the tubes then. I was clueless. I still have problems now and I've lived in London for a while. We did get on the wrong tube going the wrong way a couple of times but in true Nand and Alan style we wet ourselves laughing about it rather than stress.

As we were travelling around, we were starting to realise there was no way we were making all the appointments. London is a nightmare to get around, everything takes ten times longer than usual and I hadn't factored this in. We had to look at the list and have a chat about where we could cancel. Where was too far out the way, where was not quite appropriate. We got it down to around five and they were all completely different.

The tropical wind tunnel near the O2 was fascinating but there is no way you could put an exhibition of clothing in it and whilst it was lovely to visit, we realised straight away it was a no.

Hoxton Basement was really what it said on the tin but the photos they had on their website were amazing. When we got there, we literally had to kick a rat out the way to get down to a piss smelling basement dungeon, not something for the exhibition.

The Mermaid was lush and thank God we went to see it. Up until this point I think Nand and I were starting to lose hope. The problem is there was building works going on and whilst we loved the building, the location and possibly the space we couldn't actually see the room and I wasn't convinced it was big enough for what we wanted.

The Tobacco Docks were amazing, and we went here

straight after The Mermaid and all of a sudden, we had two real contenders for a venue. The venue itself was a massive L shaped room and we could picture straight away where stages would go and how it could be laid out. They were both coming in around the same budget and I was sure I could get the quotes down more.

At the end of the second day we had managed to get the list down to a clear 2 front runners. We still had the following morning to go and view a couple more venues and I have to say at this point my fingers were firmly crossed. The venues we had shortlisted were good and all had something different but none of them had me convinced 100%.

That night we were dead on our feet and Nand had asked in a little quiet begging voice if it was ok if we just stayed in the hotel room and chilled out. Where had she been for the first 30 years of my life. It was like we were naturally on the same wavelength. Yes, please PJs on and pizza ordered.

Nand would kill me for this but one of the nicest things about that night was that Nand fell asleep before me. We'd never slept in the same room before, so I had no reason to know this. Nand has the cutest little snore ever, she was tiny in every way, but I was lying in bed actually giggling at her little cute snore, quiet like a little dormouse snoring. Cuteness. I already loved my little pink friend all the world, but it was this trip away that cemented our friendship forever. Even when we were tired and hungry and narky with each other, we handled it and moved on. There are rules for Nand, make sure she is fed, make sure she has coffee periodically and don't make her walk for miles. Like a little pink fluffy gremlin with her own set of care rules.

Even after everything we have been through with the exhibition, everything that has happened to us, I'd do it all again if we could go back to this, stop for a second and appreciate it even more than we already did at the time.

The last day in London before heading back to Coventry and then Cyprus was another early start. Up, checked out and on our way to the first of only three venues that day to fit in.

After getting the wrong train and laughing hysterically about it we eventually got to the first venue. It was a clean crisp art gallery, nothing majorly wrong with it but the location was awkward.

However, it was the very last venue that we would view that would really stick out for both of us. Keeping in mind we were exhausted, hot and whilst it had been the best fun ever it was a slog and it was telling on us both.

We got to Business Design Centre in Islington a little early strangely, so we had enough time to sit outside, take in the vibe of the area, people watch and enjoy the sunshine. It would be almost a year to the day that we would be launching the exhibition, so it was easy to see what the vibe of the area was going to be.

After signing in to the venue (something else that was a thrill as for the first time we got little sticky labels to wear with the company's name 'Spice Girls' Exhibition' on it) we were taken upstairs to view the atrium gallery rooms and to be fair on the venue, the entrance, the agricultural hall and the surroundings are pretty impressive and a little breathtaking. There is a huge expansive space that historically was used as a kind of auction space for cattle, beyond vast, with huge arched glass roofs. It was certainly unique, especially for central London.

After keeping it together and playing it business like, we walked into the atrium, had a look and when I turned to see Nand, she was emotional. Nand was standing wiping away a tear whilst whispering:

> "It's perfect."

> "Right you, we are here on business, stop crying and giving the game away, we still have to get the deal we need."

The both of us were trying to keep it together in front of Emma, the girl showing us around, but inside we were both giddy, giving each other glances and smiling whilst very officially picking holes in it. I don't think we were doing that good a job of having a poker face, the giddy kids in us were taking over.

After three days of scouting venues in every corner of London, we skipped out of the Business Design Centre knowing that we had found a perfect venue for us providing we could get the quote right, providing the numbers worked out. The numbers that would eventually be our curse. The venue, whilst trying to get us to secure the exhibition failed to mention all of the additional costs and *if only* we had known this at this point, I would have walked away from it.

Nand and I continued to chat about the venues and it was a few weeks before we would make the final decision and decide that we definitely wanted the Business Design Centre. The Tobacco Docks were still in the game as was The Mermaid.

Looking back now, we had never made it a secret to any of the venues that it was a private collection and we had a tight budget, and I am sure the BDC left out half of the costs and charges on purpose to get ahead of the game. Other venues were quoting us inclusive of everything; security, electricity, all of the running costs. The BDC gave us this impression and then slowly started adding in any additional charges that they could. More about that later....

All in all, the trip to London was a huge success. Not only that but I feel like Nand and I really cemented our friendship over these few days. A close friend had now become a best friend and together we had the most fun ever, nothing was ever too serious.

Back in Cyprus is where the real work would need to begin. I had the front runners for the venue, it was now time to crunch the numbers, work on the plan and see how we could take it forward further.

5

Planning London

The power of positive thinking is real, and I have loved learning about it from Nand and Stevie C. I've also loved the changes it has made to my life since putting it into practice. They've taught me what is worth stressing about and what you really just need to let go. You can't control everything, but you can try your hardest to create your vision and make your dreams come true.

Nand and Stevie C (more so Stevie C) truly believed that London was the place to be and stay. Stevie C was convinced and still is, that a permanent Spice Girls' exhibition in London would be a huge success with the tourist market. I think he might be right but unfortunately that is not a road I will be walking down anytime soon.

There was so much to plan that, other than the venue, it was hard to know where to start. Although I had already created an exhibition previously, it felt like I was starting all over again. It hadn't worked in Cyprus and if I couldn't make it work this time then it was the end of the dream. We decided very early on with London that it was make or break. If we couldn't make it work in London then we couldn't make it work. All or nothing!

It was so exciting and even with all the challenges, I had been desperate to get going with it all properly. What I have failed to mention at this point is that whilst I was in London scouting venues with Nand and having a great time, poor Steven was out working in Afghanistan, trying hard to make money to get us back on an even keel. I missed him so much and it was taking its toll on me a little bit and of course, as if I could add to his worries. The one person who I usually told I was low, the one person who always knew how to make me laugh or cuddle me until it was okay, was away from me and had his own problems like bloody bombs going off and dodging rockets!

That combined with medical issues I was having with my thyroid and with other things (again another book, mostly body image), life was frustrating me lots. Steven wasn't around to calm me down. I was stressed about his safety. We were still picking ourselves up. My cat was sick (and died). But worst of all and this was definitely the worst of it, my doctor, who I had trusted, was actually lying through his teeth about treatment that he had promised me. We had worked on a treatment plan together for years, which included losing weight and stopping smoking, and after I had achieved all of that he denied all knowledge. Years of hard work and determination to get to where I needed to be for surgery. I get the surgery referral from my specialist and the scumbag doctor lies. Not only does he lie but he continues to do so, even until this day. This had an incredible impact on my mental health, more so than I realised at the time, resulting in a total breakdown.

My love affair with the island of Cyprus ended quite badly. I'd sold off my business so was no longer running around like crazy. Steven was away. My doctor was lying (for whose conduct I have since had an apology from the military surgeon general about). It's not worth it for me to name him but Mike Simms, karma is a bitch! (Changed my mind about naming the scumbag!)

One thing I am always good at is putting a brave face on. I don't like people to see me hurting, wounded or down on my luck. I like to present a happy-go-lucky kind of person. Life is too short to be too serious all the time.

Alex M, my amazing designer started working on the project a little bit again and together we came up with a plan for sponsorships for London. We had tried and failed to break through in Cyprus, but we were confident that we could attract some high-end sponsorship this time and with an ever-growing social media following, it certainly proved a lot easier at the start. I did know that it had been drummed home that there was no way in the world we were going to be funding this completely on our own, we couldn't. If the exhibition was going to have any chance at all we had to secure funding for it.

Determined to learn from our mistakes I started researching corporate sponsorship and how best to secure backing. It wasn't long until I stumbled across a company called Slingshot Sponsorship and even more so their Managing Director and the owner of the company, Jackie Fast.

Jackie Fast according to online information about her is a leading industry expert who had just won an award for her outstanding achievements in the industry, the Emerging Leaders Award (EMEA) 2017 and Slingshot sponsorship were nominated for four ESA Excellence Awards 2017 (although Jackie Fast is now the chair of these awards, so I am unsure of their relevance or meaning).

I was nervous to pick up the phone to Slingshot. It was essential to the project that we secured the funding that we needed, without it there was no exhibition. We had a very limited budget to get the project off the ground, it would need to be our own cash to get the ball rolling, Jackie was made aware of this from our very first chat. It was a passion project but in order to get it off the ground sponsorship was the key.

No need to be nervous, it wasn't like some big company where it was difficult to get through to the person you want to talk to, I called and by luck (good or bad) Jackie answered. After introducing myself and explaining what I was doing with the Spice

Girls' Exhibition, I was greeted by a crazy fangirl reaction and this would become standard when talking about the exhibition in London.

Screams of excitement mixed with:

> "Oh my God, I used to dress up as a Spice Girl when I was a little girl, I am a huge fan, I can't wait to be involved with this."

> "Like, do you actually have the costumes they have worn?"

Proper fangirl material where Jackie couldn't have made it clearer how much she wanted to work on the project, how much of a Spice Girls' fan she was and how she couldn't wait to hear about all the costumes and see them all.

> "Can I try them on?"

As usual I was ambitious and wanting to achieve as much as we possibly could with it, but in order to do that I needed a budget. After sending slingshot our initial sponsorship packages, headline sponsor £100,000, VIP sponsor £30,000 and so on, the total for the packages was well over £300,000. Whilst we knew it was incredibly ambitious, even if we secured half of that we would have an incredible exhibition.

Jackie came back to me and said that we had done well as independents, but they needed to put a professional spin on it. Although it needed some work done to it and our packages were a little overpriced, they were more than confident that they could secure what we needed.

Nothing was too much for Jackie and within a week I had a whole reworked package of sponsorship that she thought in her "expert opinion" was perfectly priced. The next step was to meet up and talk it through, listen to the pitch, see what they could do for us and put pen to paper.

Another trip to London was required, but more about this in a minute.

Happy in the belief that I had at least secured a working partnership with one of, if not the top sponsorship company and happy with the belief that they knew what they were doing. Well, according to their online profile and the boasts of all the awards they and indeed Jackie were winning. I was satisfied I'd done my research and found the right person for the job and turned my attention to other aspects of the exhibition.

Promoting and marketing, the layout, how it would work in the space, the launch evening, it all seemed so exciting and it all seemed to be going to plan perfectly. It was different to Cyprus. I wasn't having to kick down doors in the same way to get people to believe in it. This was London, the home of the Spice Girls. It wasn't a hard sell. It wasn't hard to get people excited about the costumes and memorabilia. Nothing like Cyprus.

Still negotiating with the venue and nothing signed in concrete we still didn't have anything guaranteed and were originally looking at dates in August leading into September. However, these dates were coming in at over £120,000 for the venue alone. See if you use a business style venue in the summer when it is not at its peak demand in the city you can supposedly get a much better deal. Same goes with corporate advertising on tube lines, in newspapers and anywhere else really.

By moving the dates of the exhibition slightly we could cut the cost considerably and from an initial quote of £120,000 from the venue, others like The Mermaid were coming in at around 80k so it wasn't overly ridiculous but we managed to get the quote down to £51k which we later got down to £41k because of ridiculous building works to take place during the run. Even if we secured only half the sponsorship that Slingshot were talking about, I was more than confident the venue costs were covered.

It's hard to start a business or an event when you don't actually have much capital to invest. What I did have was this huge Spice Girls' collection, most of the display aids needed to show the collection, the initial programme from Cyprus, the blueprint and marketing material of how it looked on show and of course oodles of passion for the project.

The photos and material that we had from the Cyprus exhibition became our selling point for London. It was much easier to sell an event that already had a blueprint, that already had pictures showing exactly how it would work laid out. Cyprus had many things we could have changed but these pictures and promo material that we had were now opening all sorts of doors for us according to Jackie.

The other thing that made London a little bit easier workwise for me was that all the written curation had already been done. The timeline of history was written for Cyprus. All of the research and fact checking had been done for the Cyprus programme. It was already curated and just need a few tweaks here and there.

I was back to having a total buzz about the project through the most difficult of personal turmoil. On one hand I had a nice settled life, friends and a lot to look forward to and on the other hand I was going through mental health hell. Total anxiety breakdown.

I was trained to help children label and identify their feelings and work their way through them. I did this every day at work for years, helping others handle anxieties and issues and yet for some reason in myself I couldn't identify that I was having a breakdown. I couldn't identify that the problems I was having with my doctor were taking their toll on me massively and I couldn't see that my thyroid and Grave's Disease was having a huge impact on my levels of anxiety. Anxiety that I couldn't label. I'd had depression before, and anxiety associated with it but never had I had anxiety lead depression and it snuck up on me. I could deal with mental health issues. I had always had problems but never since I was 15 years old did I try and kill myself.

I had the usual teenage angst and situations to deal with but for some reason I let it get to me more than others, as a child and a teenager I let these childhood anxieties take me to really dark places, places where I would hurt myself and more than that try and kill myself. Nothing is worth this and I wish I could go back and shake my childhood self or at least get the help that I needed.

Back to adulthood, I was so ashamed and felt like my whole mental health fight for years was back to zero. That I had relapsed completely, and I hadn't even noticed that it was happening still shocks me as I am writing this. It had crept up on me so silently, so quickly and like a series of dominos. I was fighting to make life better to try and turn things around and sort the issues we had, paddling like hell under the surface and putting on a brave face to the people I should have been asking for help. But it wasn't working.

I don't have a clue how it got this point or what even happened in the lead up to it happening. I am sure it was a phone call from the medical centre that tipped me over the edge but..

I am so sorry to say that I put a noose around my neck. I thought it through and planned it before, it wasn't a spur of the moment drunken thing that just happened. Why did I not stop at any single point along the thought process and ask for help? There must have been people I had seen that day that I could have just said help me to. This isn't who I am as an adult and looking back it is really easy to label it up as a full-blown mental health breakdown.

There was a note written, the dogs were locked away, the attic was open and I knew exactly what I was going to tie the flex to. I'd brought through the stool from the dressing table to put on the bed so that I could reach up into the attic and then I drank myself stupid.

At any point I could and should have stopped. I should have asked for help. I should have committed myself to hospital or done absolutely anything else.

As I stepped up on that stool my balance was obviously drunk, I fell and hurt my wrist before I could attach the flex to the rafters in the attic and as I lay on the single bed in the spare bedroom under the open attic hatch, I was broken, a sobbing howling mess of a man at absolute rock bottom.

It truly was like I had been hit with a train, I lay there and cried myself to sleep. The next morning I woke up feeling so hungover and sick but when I tried to run to the toilet to throw up, I tripped on the noose that was still around my neck and nearly broke my neck as I smacked my head on the wall. It would have served me bloody right for being so fucking stupid.

I didn't make it to the toilet to be sick and ended up lying on the floor with sick all over the wall, the floor, in my hands and with my head thumping even more now than it was when I first came to. Again, serves me right, as you can probably tell I am really annoyed with myself for this. I wish I had told someone how I was feeling. I wish I'd said to any single one of my friends anywhere in the world, but I didn't and instead I lay there with tears stinging my face and the sound of the dogs whining from the other bedroom.

The thing about having an episode like this is, it is very very sobering, I'd been here before but a long time ago and I knew from experience that this is rock bottom. It doesn't matter what happens now I'd already hit my rock bottom. My rock bottom was sitting there in my own vomit with a makeshift noose around my neck, tears streaming down my face, my dogs (that I'd selfishly locked away) whining in the other bedroom, the attic hatch lying open and my head absolutely splitting every time my heart made a beat.

Everything after this is a complete blur for weeks. I don't remember any sequence of events really or how it got to a stage where I told people what had actually happened. I think I was shell shocked and after telling Nand eventually, she said she knew something had happened. It's all a huge blur and of course it is hard to talk and write about it.

The worst moment of my adult life, I think in the long run, will become one of the most defining and profound moments of my life.

I wrote an email about the impact the doctor lying

was having on me, it had pushed me over the edge. All I had ever done was follow his instructions in a path of care for us to get to the last hurdle before the surgery I needed, and he lied about it all. All over funding and a change to the Colonel in charge. It literally tipped me over the edge, and I found myself in the deepest darkest hole I'd ever been in.

Karma is a bitch and I believe one day this man will get what he deserves. I begged and pleaded with him to tell the truth. I told him that if he did the right thing, I would let everything slide and forget about all the lies he was telling. He ignored it and thought he was untouchable. Brushed me aside despite knowing comprehensively the impact it was having on my mental health. The man is vile.

Anyway, from rock bottom there is only really one way you can go and that is up. And from experience not only will I fight back, but I will come back even stronger and more determined than ever before, but at this point I had to be honest.

I sent the email to three people in my life. I needed help. I needed people to know I was not okay. I needed help desperately and I was scared about what would happen if I didn't scream for that help.

I sent the email to Steven, to my mum and to Nand. I'm not sure when that was, as in whether it was a day after, a week after or two weeks after, again the whole timeframe is a blur. Up until the actual point of sending the email I don't really know how I'd got there.

I don't remember what the email says or when I wrote it, I don't really want to read it ever again.

I don't think I'll ever remember beyond having a shower that morning and Nand walking into my house with flowers, giving me the biggest hug ever, breaking our hearts together and then Nand hitting me and being a bit upset with me.

My mum was heartbroken and so was Steven, they knew I had been struggling but I don't think anyone knew just how badly things were affecting me and just how much it had all got on top of me.

From that moment though I started to get better, and I still continue to get better every day.

Throwing myself into the whole #SpiceUpLondon organising was a natural distraction but I couldn't have even begun to do that if it hadn't been for some serious chats with my Steven, my Nand and my mum, but above that there was one person who took me aside and who showed me something that changed my life.

Grandad took me aside one night and showed me a documentary, well not so much a documentary but what could be termed as a psychobabble film concentrating on the laws of the universe. The law of attraction and what you put out in life you get back.

The thing is, that along with a pep talk about how I was constantly angry and frustrated with the situation, I was wasting so much energy being angry and upset that it was a vicious circle. Stevie C, in his kitchen in Cyprus, single-handedly persuaded me to let it go. Let it fucking go and don't let it eat you up.

Chill out and look for the positive in every single situation, put out positive vibes and that is exactly what you get in return. This has changed my life. From this moment I took control of everything that I could take control of and anything I couldn't control, I stopped worrying about and started to look for alternative options.

It makes sense to me and I bought into it wholeheartedly. I needed something to believe in and this was something I could put into practice with immediate effect, and I did.

I don't just think this has changed my life but it has also changed our relationship and how Steven is in life. Steven couldn't quite deal with the changes in me at first, he was used to me moaning and being angry and now I was a lot more mellow and chilled about everything in general. Not only that, but I stopped allowing him to moan about everything. I love my Steven all the world but we both got into a rut where the glass was half empty and when I started actively doing the opposite, it was a big change to deal with. I honestly believe we are both much happier for it.

Planning stages were well under way at this point and one of my favourite parts of any project is the initial drawing, sketching, mind mapping and everything else that goes along with it. I have folders and folders of sketches from different projects over the years. Moulin Rouge costumes from an amateur production, stage designs from panto sets, sketches of the Cyprus exhibition and now designs of the London exhibition.

In total, I think by the end of London, we had gone through an incredible eight A4 refill pads of paper, a huge number of notes, calculations and everything else you could possibly imagine. The project was so big that there was no way it was a one-man project and there was absolutely no way I was able to keep it all in my brain.

Another legitimate way of raising funds for a start-up project is things like crowdfunding. However, of course with me it was never going to be that simple and there were people who were uneducated who did what they always do and ridiculed what I was doing with crowdfunding.

As well as obtaining sponsorships, offering people the chance to attend the launch evening, book tickets in advance, reserve programmes and other rewards are genuine crowdfunding techniques used to help get projects off the ground.

Without the initial crowdfunding and then later crowdfunding for the Spice Bus, the project wouldn't even have got off the ground. So, to those people who took a leap of faith and backed me right at the start, thank you very much! Not only did your pledge help get the project started but your belief in me is what spurred me on when others were constantly telling me to give up.

6

Party Central

I had been working in the primary school on base for nearly four years and this it in itself was a massive dream come true and privilege. I seemed to take to working as a classroom assistant like a duck to water and of course I made some amazing friends. Fay and I worked together for a couple of years and I think they only split us up because other people were feeling left out. We had become a great team that had amazing ways of bending the rules and making education as fun as we possibly could for the children.

Unfortunately, after working with an amazing little boy called Connor (Hi Connor, hope you like the mention buddy) it was clear that the school had failed him time after time. Excluded 17 times in a year at 6 years old, something is going really wrong. I couldn't stay in the job. I was so unhappy not to be able to do my job to the fullest of my ability due to bloody bureaucratic red tape nonsense and others not doing their jobs properly. In a small environment like the base it is hard not to make friendships and develop loyalties, but loyalties and fear of acting should not impact on children.

For the last six months of my job in the school I had been working at the weekends as an entertainer, singing in local bars, hotels and restaurants. I'd also been asked to help out at a children's birthday party and it was here that I realised there was a real gap in the market for children's parties both on the base and the surrounding areas in Cyprus. I also quickly realised that it was impossible to get balloons, fancy dress costumes or themed party wear.

Before I knew it, I was arranging children's birthday parties, making party bags, playing party games, hiring face painters and all sorts. Then, on the other hand, I was ordering fancy dress costumes in time for Halloween, party wear to offer themed kids' parties and anything else associated with parties or celebrations.

I started selling the items online at first, through Facebook groups, local fetes and of course word of mouth. The nearest fancy dress shop to where we lived was at least an hour's drive away so the demand for the costumes was high and there were people turning up at the house at all hours of the day to pick up costume orders, pay for parties and God knows what else.

It got a little bit much and a little became a lot of invasion of privacy. I like to keep myself to myself when I am at home and the door is closed, it's our time and people really were turning up at all hours.

Balloons were hard to get a hold of in Cyprus but not only that they were so incredibly expensive that even if people did figure out where to get them, they normally decided against it because of the price.

Watching YouTube tutorials, I quickly taught myself how to make balloon structures such as archways, castles and themed balloon stands. They were incredibly popular, and it was a perfect addition to the business as a whole.

The other issue with running a business from home is that it takes over your entire house and before long every single room in the house with the exception of our bedroom had something related to the business in it. Time to get a shop.

Steven wasn't convinced about the Party Central Shop at first but before long he had the notion of owning a chain of them on the island and staying in Cyprus forever, maybe that was a better plan than what we actually did, ha!

The shop was an amazing little addition to the business, as well as being able to stock everything you need to party it was also a place where people could come and discuss their event and what they needed.

Within a year of setting the business up I was running most of the children's parties on both the local military bases as well as making roads into the Cypriot market. It wasn't just a case of running the parties, we provided everything from the entertainment, mascot appearances, face painters and clowns to party food, gift bags, wrapped party prizes and loads more. It was a one stop party shop, but bloody hell it was a lot of work.

Steven was working full-time during the week in his job and then at nights and at the weekends was helping me run parties and everything else that went with it.

What we didn't quite factor in when getting the shop is that someone would actually have to be there all the time to man it and it was becoming a bit of a pain to have to be there all the time. It was amazing to have a base and it made so much money at certain times of the year but every single day, whether I felt like it or not, I'd have to go and open the shop.

It did become a working office as well and it was a God send for the beginning of the planning for London. I had to get up and go and open the shop and therefore whether I wanted to be or not I was out the house, at work and getting on with planning, not just the business but the exhibition.

The only time the shop was ever closed for any length of time was during the #SpiceUpCyprus exhibition. There was just no way that we could run an exhibition seven days a week as well as run the shop and the children's parties. We were a good team but there are limitations to what two people can do.

There were a lot of 4am starts and 2am finishes and

there were times where we would get home from a gig on a Sunday morning at 2am to then have to get up at 4.30am to start cooking for a party or to get the party bags ready. Looking back, I don't have a clue how we managed to keep up this pace of life, but we did and most of the time in scorching heat.

When the Cyprus exhibition went wrong and we realised it had cost us so much money, the only thing that really kept us going was the fact that we still had Party Central. I still had the shop; all the stock and we were more popular than ever with parties and gigs.

A regular Saturday could look like this: 5am start to cook food, make up party bags and wrap prizes, one of us would go to the shop to open up and one of us would head off to the first party of the day, sometimes a little beach DJ'ing gig for Steven. Then it would be a second kids' party with the gorgeous Emma, who was my bestest little helper for most of the time owning Party Central. Maybe a third party of the day, balloons for Saturday evening events and then home to get ready for a night-time gig.

Repeat on Sunday.

It was a crazy lifestyle and it was burn out, collapse in a heap on the floor material, but we thrived. The times we didn't thrive are when we were exhausted on two hours' sleep, throwing up and narking at each other.

A massive bonus to it all of course was the money

that we were able to make and there were weekends where we had big events on with balloons and everything else that we could take home a few thousand euros at the end of it.

When the Cyprus exhibition went wrong and we were left with all of this crazy debt both with local companies and with Steven's dad, Party Central Cyprus was the way we could make it right.

We threw ourselves into the work and began slowly chipping away at the debt from local companies, to pay Liz for some of the costumes and to try and get ourselves to some kind of even keel.

When the exhibition went wrong, we decided we had to sell the gorgeous Jeep that we had and trade it in for an old banger as long as it was big enough to carry the business stuff like speakers etc. We cut back everything that we could and really had to live to a very tight budget.

Through sheer hard work and determination, we got there with most of the money that we owed, except for Steven's dad, we managed to get ourselves back on track, an even keel and even managed to invest in more costumes and memorabilia at the same time.

After dusting ourselves off and picking ourselves up off the floor, fighting back in any and every way that we knew how to, we were tired, and we also knew that our time in Cyprus was coming to an end with Steven's contract up soon.

We decided that the best course of action was to sell off Party Central Cyprus after building it up to be a known brand for entertainment and events on the island of Cyprus. We tried to sell it as a whole business, but it seemed that different people were interested in different aspects of it.

We sold off the party side with the business licence for the bases to Emma, who had been amazing when working with us, she also bought some of the DJ'ing and lighting equipment that we had amassed. Nobody wanted to take on the shop, so we sold off all of the stock to different people around the island.

It didn't make us millionaires by a long shot, but it was enough to tide me along for the 10 months or so that I had left on the island. It also allowed me to turn my attention almost full-time on the planning of the new #SpiceUpLondon exhibition. Something that even from the start we knew had to be bigger and better than what we had created in Cyprus.

The spanner in the works was that not long after we had sold off Party Central Cyprus and decided to take things at a slower pace for our remaining time in Cyprus, Steven got offered a job in Afghanistan. The story is maybe a little back to front with this covered in the previous chapter, but it felt more natural to write it like this.

By the time Steven went to Afghanistan I was already full-time on planning for London, it was going to be a whole new start for us. We should have been able to pay his dad off in full and have a little extra money left over for ourselves. As usual we always plan well, it just doesn't always work out that way for us. There is always some hurdle to get over first.

Looking back now, Party Central Cyprus along with so many other things we achieved together whilst in Cyprus, is one of the things that I am proudest of in life. I spotted a gap in the market but not only that, I filled it with quality and reliable entertainment, something that was rare in Cyprus. The reason I had decided to run children's parties on the base was because I worked with these children in the schools and before we started Party Central what they were getting was some 30 something year old guy turning up either hungover or coked out his nut to run their parties. They deserved better, and with my background working with kids I knew I could do a better job than that clown.

It became more than that though. It became something we were incredibly proud to put our name to, people from all over the island were hiring us but we were also making inroads into the Cypriot families and that was true praise. Even with the language barrier, we were their best option for fun.

Never underestimate fun.

Passing the baton over for Party Central wasn't easy especially given that I had promised a better service to the kids of the base, but it was made easier passing it over to Little Em knowing that we had fun doing it. We had fun interacting with people at their special occasions and I was satisfied that out of nothing I had established a successful little business for myself.

The shop made a small fortune at certain times of the year, the children's parties were a regular fixture, I had live singing gigs on a weekly basis and Steven had DJ'ing gigs booked months in advance. Through hard work and the determination to fight back we created a little cracker of a business and whilst it was time to move on from it there is a part of me that would have been happy to stay and run the business for a few more years at least.

7

Another New Adventure

It's really hard for me to write about the last few months in Cyprus before we moved back to Liverpool. Partly due to the fact that I had a complete mental breakdown, but also partly down to the fact that it was so busy, so crammed packed with events, that it all blurs into one big fuzzy moving picture.

One of the last amazing things that we did do before moving back was renewing our wedding vows on a beach next to where we lived. With Nand and Stevie C there as best man and woman, Emma and Neil as photographers and friends and the gorgeous Jaime Barber as our officiator it was only the seven of us with a beautiful Cyprus sunset, the waves on the beach, flip flops on our feet and bottles of champagne that had been gifted to us over our time in Cyprus. I had a gorgeous bouquet of flowers, which whilst simple was so significant to me. I'd never been allowed a bouquet at our first wedding.

The whole thing was so significant for me in so many different ways. It was the perfect way for us to say goodbye to the beautiful island that had been our home for the past six years, after being apart for a while (which we had never done before) and with Steven having to go back out to Afghanistan for a second stint it felt perfect. We also had the party of all parties as we hired the VIP balcony of one of the biggest beach clubs in Europe, Guaba, and had a great evening with our Cyprus family. Most importantly though, it really felt like a new start for me. I felt like I'd let my Steven down by letting myself get so low and not telling him about it. Standing on that beach, telling him how much I loved him, made me realise just how lucky I was to have him

He, of course, had to go back to Afghanistan to finish his tour, but he was enjoying the tour in a way and now that I really was on the mend and trying hard to turn my life around completely, I was happy for him to go on his adventure.

It left me to once again (Steven is an expert at this) to pack up the house and get us all ready to move back to our new home, which was going to be in Liverpool. The hometown of Sporty Spice, I was excited about it, a new adventure for us.

The Military packers are amazing, so that side of it is was made easy for me. All of our personal items, that we would be taking back with us such as furniture, paintings etc, were all packed up and shipped back for us. All I had to do was be in the house and make sure it was only items we wanted to go that were packed away. The guys were slick at their job and checked off every single item they had put into the boxes.

Moving the collection back was a whole different story, Big Dave who I had become friends with and who was also best friends with Nand and Stevie C, had brought the collection over for me. I love Dave but I have two nicknames for him, Superhero Dave and Diva Dave. Superhero Dave because he goes out of his way to be helpful for people but at the same time overstretches himself and then as a result can let people down timescale wise, he's always chasing his own arse. I can imagine being in the pub and someone saying they needed a fridge moved, Dave ripping his shirt open to reveal a superhero logo and shouting

"Motha Fucka, Superhero Dave can fix it"

'Diva Dave' is kind of self-explanatory, I've never known a big hairy-arsed brick shit house of a man to bitch and moan about life as much as Diva Dave does.

My first issue with Dave was initially quoting me 5k to ship the collection to Cyprus from Glasgow. He then spent the next three months telling me not to worry he has got it much cheaper than that and it should be around £3K, but he would have the final figure for me 'soon'. Diva Dave then handed me an invoice for just over £5K. If he'd stuck to his original quote I could have shopped around and done my homework, I'd probably have gone to him anyway but, instead he spent months promising to get me it for less, but when it came down to the number crunching he couldn't and had over promised. Not out of badness but out of trying to keep me happy.

It was a bit farcical at times with clerical errors costing money and delays at the ports and, of course, even though I'd never had anything to do with the forms the clerical error was my mistake and not Diva's.

At the end of the day Dave, my big daft buddy, managed to get the collection to Cyprus safely, not only that but he bent over backwards to help in any way he could. He moaned like fuck about it, but he still puts a lot of effort in the big softy.

On the way back it was easier just to get Dave to sort it for us again. We didn't have an exact address sorted as of yet so it was easier to work with him with that than it would have been with anyone else. Dave and I have always been able to rut heads and get over it, but I would say moving the collection back from Cyprus put that to a test with both of us being equally as pissed off with each other.

Dave has a memory like a sieve due to the fact that he is always so busy. As a result, he forgets what he has said or promised and then just makes up his own gospel truth about it.

The collection going back to Liverpool was a bit of a nightmare from start to finish but again we got there in the end with it, although I'm not sure we are still buddies?

The boxes and some of the items like the motorbike were left uncovered either in the port at Cyprus or in the warehouse in Liverpool, as a result every single box and some of the items were absolutely caked in bird shit and the first thing we had to do when we picked up most of the boxes was go and buy new containers to put it all in. Who bloody knew plastic storage boxes were so expensive?

Anyway, despite the usual dramas involved with Diva we managed to get the collection home, fitting it and all the mannequins and two motorbikes, around 40 boxes of memorabilia, dolls, awards, and everything else into a three-bedroom semi with no garage was going to be a bit of a squeeze and it was!

With the collection on its way back and with the house stuff on its way back as well, it was now up to me to sell everything else off.

The cars, the couches, the swimming pool, the jacuzzi and anything else that wasn't going back. This was fun and I loved sorting it all out and selling it all off. Again, I think it was a little bit therapeutic to cleanse our life of everything that we had amassed in six years in Cyprus.

With Steven not due back until the end of October and with us moving on the 7th November it was a bit of a tough job trying to get everything sorted. We were moving to a new city that we had only ever visited for the weekend and we had no way of knowing even what area to live in and what area to avoid.

Our friends soon let us know when we posted about possibly having a new house in a certain area. Our joy was short-lived when we found out it wasn't ideal for us. We eventually found a little house after a lot of arguments with letting agents. Who knew it could be so hard to rent a house from someone, there are no exceptions made for anyone or circumstances!

The rules were if I wanted to rent a house, I had to turn up in person to view it and present my passport in person.

In October I flew back for a few days and decided again to try and cram as much in as I could. It would get a lot easier to get to meetings etc. when we were back in Liverpool but for now, I really had to try and get as much done as possible whilst in the UK.

I viewed the house in the Wirral and instantly loved it, it wasn't our four-bedroom detached house in Cyprus with a swimming pool and views to die for, but it was very homely and cosy. I just had no idea how we were possibly going to fit everything in.

Travelling to Liverpool on my own was exciting and after signing for the house in the afternoon I made my way into the city and met up with my buddy Josh for a few pints. I always have fun with Josh. He is another of my besties and we sang together in an acoustic duo in Cyprus for a while. It was nice to get a catch up, but rather like me Josh wears his heart on his sleeve when he is drinking, so you always get an honest chat and opinion. He has an old wise head on his shoulders (SOMETIMES), and I have grown to really value his opinion and so we ended up with a proper therapeutic heart to heart.

The next day I made my way down to London again and had a few meetings lined up to chat about all things #SpiceUpLondon. As I sat on the train on the way to London, I couldn't actually believe that this dream, this pipe dream was now becoming a reality. My brain was swamped with thoughts of what we could do, how it could look.

I had a meeting with Ticketmaster and I absolutely loved walking in that building and seeing all the different ticket stubs up on the wall. Of course, I was able to spot the Spice Girls' tickets instantly, something the guys from Ticketmaster were impressed with, strangely.

With the tickets platform and sales sorted in theory, through a new self-service ticketing platform called Universe, I really was talked into this, I wasn't convinced at the time and I am still not convinced it was the right platform. What I will say is the guys from Universe were incredibly patient with us and by the end of the journey we genuinely thought a lot of each other.

Meetings with Slingshot Sponsorship and the venue were next, Slingshot rented an office in the Business Design Centre, so it really was ideal to have them in the same location.

This was the first time I was introduced in person to Jackie Fast and Kieran from Slingshot. Jackie was well dressed, well-groomed and came across as lovely at first. Kieran whilst a little bit on the hunky side, was quiet and you could see straight away he was dominated by Jackie, seeking her approval with almost every sentence.

Jackie tried to present as sweet and nicey nice, but you can see through people like that straight away. A pretence doesn't last, and it wasn't long until Jackie was trying to be fierce and dominate the whole meeting.

Her take on it was that we need to:

> "Strike whilst the iron is hot, this is the time when companies are investing, I need you to sign in now if we have any hope of getting it all secured before the Christmas break."

This along with numerous other sentences of this kind such as:

> "We have a big client interested so it's not going to be hard to secure significant backing."

With the reassuring conversations we were having about the exhibition and what we had to offer, there was one of the "leading industry experts" so confident that she could secure what we needed that she put a sale deadline of the 24th November.

It was going to cost me £3,000 a month to employ

Jackie and Slingshot. I'd checked all their credentials and they checked out. I had absolutely no reason not to believe that they could pull it off and in fact I skipped out of the office, into the sunshine and gave a huge sigh of relief. All was going to be okay and we would have all the funding we needed. Now I could plough on with the business of planning.

Heading back to Cyprus for the last month of our tour there, I was feeling like the cat that had got the cream. Everything was falling into place nicely and it wasn't long until I had my Steven back from Afghanistan and we'd be off on a brand-new adventure to Liverpool.

It was amazing to finally have Steven back and I vowed then never to let him go away from me ever again. I'd missed him so much and I had no idea that it was that bad. I've always liked my own space and liked to think of myself as independent, but not now. I need Steven and I'm not scared to admit that. He is my rock and always tries his hardest to do the best by me and pick me up when I am down.

The one thing that was a little bit sad about leaving Cyprus, apart from leaving behind some amazing friends, was that our little pussycat we had taken with us wasn't making it back with us, two new naughty beagles were though.

Getting them ready and handing them over to be shipped back was horrendous. You wouldn't just hand your kids over to some random and hope to see them at the other side, so it was hard to do it with the dogs.

Diva Dave helped us ship the dogs back and he was amazing with this. Dave had previously worked as a dog trainer in the military, so I knew they were in good hands with him and that he genuinely cared whether they got back safely.

The other nice thing about this was that Dave is a mate and I think we maybe got a lot more updates about their journey and progress than he would have given any other customer. He knew how worried I was and was in touch constantly when he knew what was going on.

Actually leaving Cyprus was hard, my love affair with the island was over and after the last year of medical problems I was relieved to be putting it behind me, but it was a bit of a different feeling at the airport.

I couldn't let this arsehole doctor taint my memories of the amazing six-year adventure that we had living on a military base on the beautiful sunshine island. The memories we had of performing on stage in pantos and musicals, the memories of gigging in hotels and running children's parties. The friends we had made were friends for life and all of that was golden, precious and money can't buy, time well spent.

Flying home was an experience in itself. I'd never flown from or to a military airport and it was definitely different from a large commercial airport. We checked in with almost 80kg of luggage and we were a bit worried we were going to have to leave half of our stuff behind. After a bit of banter with the check in girl she saw the funny side of it. She said there had been other people leaving with that much luggage, but it was normally families of four! Ooops!

Our friend Becca picked us up at the other side and gave us a lift to the car rental place to pick up our car and even after getting lost a couple of times on the way it wasn't long until we were in Liverpool and getting to our new home.

That night, our first night in our new house, was probably the coldest night I have had in my life. Bearing in mind that we had just been living in a hot country for six years, trying to get warm lying cuddled up on the living room floor in front of the fire, it wasn't working, and I think I got about an hour's sleep.

The new bed arrived first thing the next morning. Yes!

It wasn't long until Liverpool became home, and we settled in nicely. The only real issue was that the house was a lot smaller and we really did struggle to fit everything in. The attic was jam-packed to the extent that absolutely nothing else would fit in to it and I was a bit worried about the roof falling down.

Liverpool, well actually the Wirral became our home very quickly and we loved living there. We may only have lived there for around eight months, but we made a lot of nice memories in that house together.

The other thing that was great was that it was smack bang in the middle of the country, easy for me to go to Glasgow to see friends and easy to go to London for meetings. It was sheer luck that Steven got a job in Liverpool and that is where we moved to, but it worked out perfectly for a time.

Steven wasn't happy with his job and again it seemed to work out well for us in the long run. I had been looking at renting a flat in London for two months for the duration of the exhibition and the lead up to it, and it was expensive. Instead, Steven got a new job, London-based and so it wasn't long until we were on the move again.

I try never to go back in life, well not for any long period of time, but I would definitely move back to the Wirral again, I feel like we never got the time to fully appreciate it for the amazing place it is.

8

Always a Drama

Liverpool is really where we broke the back of the exhibition and that little house in Bebington in the Wirral was, for the time being, the SpiceUp Hub.

Even though we had chosen to employ Slingshot Sponsorship to gain us the backing that we needed this time we were leaving nothing to chance. We were making a great little team Alex and I, but it was clear by this point that we already needed more help. We were becoming swamped with list after list of things needing done.

I couldn't manage all of the social media, all of the fundraising, all of the planning, all of the sponsorship, marketing and everything else on my own.

Alex M became my full-time PA and Alex Lodge started to help out with social media, the dream team was starting to come together and every single one of us believed in the project and what we were doing.

It wasn't always plain sailing. In fact, it was far from it and we it felt like there were times we were constantly firefighting, dealing with one issue and then moving straight on to the next.

As exciting as all this was, sometimes one thing that changes and puts a whole different spin on life again.

Nand was ill again, and not for the first time, her cancer had come back, but this time it's bad.

Talking to Nand and Stevie C and her family they always had to fight, always had to believe that we could beat it with positivity, with laughter, with cannabis treatments and anything else that might have given my little pink buddy a fighting chance.

Nand was involved in the exhibition heavily, not only that but she had spurred Stevie C on to give me an initial cash investment that without it, the exhibition wouldn't have got going at all. Thanks Grandad, thanks Nand, I think you knew how much this meant to me at the time, but I am just making sure!

It was as much Nand's exhibition as it was anyone else's and every time I went to see her she would ask me what was going on, who was doing what, what was going well, what I thought I could fix. Always interested, always wanting to be kept up-to-date.

I went to stay with Nand for a day or two once a week from this point really, I couldn't not try and make the most of it and to be honest even when she was ill Nand was better company than most normal people on a good day. Even when she was sick she was a character of pink bubbly silliness.

Mixed in with all the fun and laughter that we were having, all the gossip about the exhibition, was this utter dread, this sense of complete disbelief. It's hard to remember every day-to-day detail because I was so busy, but also because I was numb, and the only way to deal with my best friend being this ill, was to shut it out.

There were moments we talked and cried but remember Nand is a funny quirky little thing and if it got too deep for too long, she farted or did something else stupid to bring the mood back round.

I don't know how I've handled it or even if I have but the one thing that I have said and I stick by is, it is hard to be sad at losing someone when you were so grateful to have them in your life at all.

We were getting busier and busier all the time with the exhibition, with meetings at the venue, meetings with the designers, meetings with the production companies, lighting companies, and with all the other partners involved.

I had arranged another quick trip to London to see the venue, have a chat about the build and timescales but also to meet with a production company called gassProductions.

I had been speaking with Andy from gass since I had been in Cyprus, my initial thought process was to try and create a documentary about the making of the exhibition, but Andy didn't quite believe in that. What he did believe in was filming some of the costumes and other items to use as promotion for the exhibition. Q & A interviews, interviews with Liz, a photo shoot in Manchester and loads more. We paid a lot for them, but I am pretty sure they did the trick with ticket sales and raising awareness.

The interesting thing about the first time I met Andy was that it was outside the Business Design Centre and I was sitting waiting for him to arrive. He was late and I wasn't impressed when it got to 15 minutes and then 20 minutes. However, there was an ambulance at the bottom of the road and I could see it from where I was sitting. Whilst he was a total geezer on the phone this guy seemed like he was genuine and interested to meet me, so I was beginning to get a little concerned that he might have had an accident.

Five minutes later and this tall skinny guy walked up the road towards me. I could just tell it was him but what the fuck, he was covered in blood. He couldn't shake my hand or anything and had to quickly excuse himself to go and get cleaned up without having a second to explain anything other than it was not his blood.

It turned out Andy needs a superhero cape (not forgotten mate), he was walking around the corner to our meeting when some poor guy on a bike started to have a seizure and fell and smacked his head. Andy has a bit of experience with epilepsy and was able to stop and help the guy until the ambulance arrived. He was holding the guy's head, which had split open on the kerb, hence the extensive blood all over him. I hope the guy was all right but from that moment I knew that Andy Smith was one of the good guys. More about him later.

Alex and I were working well together and that had been shown in the fact that we were getting breakthroughs with sponsorships on our own. Slingshot were getting nothing so far and even though they had put a deadline date of 24th November absolutely nothing was happening by that point that we hadn't created, and I mean nothing!

We had secured interest through my own social media channels and had messages back from Hilton Hotel, Tanning Salon and a few others that were interested.

I had a meeting with Hilton on this same trip down as Bloody Andy and again the guys in there couldn't have been nicer. They bent over backwards to be involved and although they were wanting to make money from our aftershow, they were also happy to support us in a room revenue share. Something that Kieran from Slingshot sponsorship tried to put a value of £100,000 on, what it really turned out to be was £148 in revenue share. Great deal, well done Kieran, we handed you a massive hotel chain that had approached us interested, and you secured us less than £200. #Proud

Such is the disgrace of Slingshot that they have a whole chapter dedicated to them coming up next.

The rest of the planning for the exhibition was going amazingly well at this point and I was becoming more and more confident with it with every ticket we sold.

It was always my intention to make London much bigger and better than Cyprus and by this point I had managed to get all of the major collectors to agree to take part and realised there was going to be at least 200 costume pieces as part of the exhibition. That in itself caused a new challenge as we would need a lot more mannequins, a lot more display aids, staging, lighting and everything else that goes along with presenting and showcasing costumes.

By the time we had secured all the mannequins we needed by the summer we were told that there was not a single black patent mannequin left available to buy in the UK, we had them all.

There was one problem at this stage and that was finances. Everyone was starting to ask for payment for things and so far, we had secured zero funds from sponsorship. This is really where issues starting creeping in, but given that we had just moved back from Cyprus and given that it was a brand-new company, it was incredibly difficult for us to secure any form of grants or business loans.

Living on the base we were supposed to still be officially on British soil and people are not meant be able to hold that against you when you get back to the UK, but try telling that to a loan adviser that doesn't recognise the postcode and just keeps repeating 'Computer says no' . The pressure at this stage was already building financially, but I managed to secure a business loan to keep us going and to started paying some of the invoices due.

Pre-ticket sales were also starting to trickle in, so this went a long way to helping us with the planning as well.

Christmas was fast approaching and of course trying to get anyone to do any work at Christmas time is a task. Everyone enters that holiday spirit and almost for the full month of December it is all about Christmas parties and lunches out.

I was becoming increasingly frustrated with the lack of progress and the lack of importance for people. As soon as Christmas was over, we were on to a seven-month countdown to the opening of the exhibition.

There was a bombshell coming, it wasn't the first bombshell and it most definitely would not be our last.........

9

Jackie Pulls a Fast One

Meeting Jackie Fast and choosing to work with Slingshot Sponsorship is the second most regrettable thing that I did with the exhibition. The first being the venue.

Jackie Fast was full of excitement for the project full of animated full on 'fangirling':

> "OMG I can't wait to see these costumes."

> "OMG I remember dressing up as ginger Spice when I was a little girl and my friends….."

Not only was she so interested in the subject, but Jackie was able to back herself up with some interesting industry awards and with some amazing write ups. I don't know what Jackie did to get these, but I doubt it had anything to do with her ability as a professional.

Here was Jackie giving us critical feedback about the packages that we had put together, adding in some content in order to capture the marketing director's attention and coming up with realistic prices for packages. The headline package was £45,000 with a sale deadline of 24th November, this deadline:

"Would push people into a sale."

In fact, I think it did the complete opposite of that. I think as soon as that deadline that they had sent out to over 200 major target companies in London had passed the whole package became un credible. They were then trying to sell clients a package that they had said should have been snapped up.

The initial contract with Slingshot sponsorship was for three months and was signed in October, the biggest surprise of all that I got from the sponsorship company when after a month and a half of promising to secure us sponsorship that we needed to make the exhibition work, a month and a half of stringing us along with exciting prospects from a lunch meeting she was attending or an exciting prospect that she had lined up at a dinner meeting. I got a message from Jackie Fast.

Jackie Pulls a Fast One:

"Dear Alan, I have sold my company Slingshot Sponsorship and will no longer be involved in your project. Please contact Kieran if you have any questions re: sponsorship."

So here is this woman who has met me in London, who has told me the importance of getting to work fast on the contracts in order to secure it before Christmas. Here is the woman who personally gave me her guarantee that she was more than confident about being able to secure the sponsorship we need, so much so that when I explained I would have to pay Slingshot out of my own pocket she said:

> "I wouldn't take your money if I couldn't do the job and I have my reputation to think of."

What an absolute crock of shit.

Jackie Fast signed us in to a three-month contract with, in my opinion, absolutely no intention of ever securing us sponsorship for the exhibition. That text message was like a punch in the guts and when I replied to her I got an undeliverable message. She had sent the text and then disconnected her phone.

I asked Kieran about Jackie and got a very vague response that she was off in Canada somewhere. The whole thing absolutely stank and I was beyond disgusted that after taking this woman at her word she couldn't have been less forthcoming.

She had obviously sold the company or at least knew the sale was coming up before signing me into a contract, these things don't happen overnight.

Now what we were left with was Kieran, and with all the will in world there is no way that Kieran was the best person ever to be working on the Spice Girls' Exhibition.

Kieran was a straight looking and acting, very straight-laced rugby playing teenager (maybe not quite a teenager) but it was just as well he was pretty to an extent, as he really wasn't always the sharpest tool in the box.

When we suggested to Kieran about contacting certain companies about sponsorships his response would be:

"Oh yeah that's a good idea."

No mate, we are paying you for you to come up with the good ideas. In fact, that's not even true either, we were paying Jackie Fast, an industry leader with awards and all sorts to her name.

The only problem with that is that Jackie Fast has pulled a fast one, sold her company and fucked off with her industry awards tucked safely under her arm, without a backwards glance or a care in the world for our project.

Of course, Kieran was never going to secure any level of sponsorship and in fact, I would say, he ended up costing us money.

The thing about Slingshot is that they kept promising that they had interest, that they had a big company ready to sign. That they were following up the leads again and again.

The only sponsorship we ever secured for the exhibition was through leads that we had generated from our social media; Hilton Hotel, Angel Islington Shopping Centre, Tanning Salons, Big Bus company.

The total sponsorship secured should have been close to £180,000, instead we managed to reach a grand total of £18,000 in paid sponsorship, all through our leads. (Not one of the paying sponsors was generated by Slingshot, Kieran or Jackie. Great work guys I can see why you are industry leaders).

10% of what we were hoping for, but the worst of it was we didn't have the time to go and start working with another sponsorship company. We were already at full stretch and Kieran was full of promises of getting something secured.

We paid Slingshot Sponsorship over 5 months' worth of contract and they were until recently still chasing my company for the rest.

£15,000 to a company who were meant to secure our future and the future of the exhibition through their profession, through what they were meant to be good at. Instead one of them has fucked off and one of them is as useful as a fart in a space suit.

The whole thing was an absolute nightmare and if it hadn't been for Alex M and Steven pulling together every aspect that we could to try and raise capital, I don't think we would have got past this stage.

The only thing that saved the whole project was the fact that I was able to get a loan from my bank for £40,000 for the company, a loan that would need to be paid back but it was enough to save the project at this time and allow us to keep going with all the plans now in place.

Despite the fact the Slingshot were not delivering

what we needed them to, and within the timescales we needed, they remained full of promises and optimism.

I remember a lunch meeting that I had with Kieran in Manchester, it must have been close to Christmas time as we were discussing the renewal of the contract. The contract had run from October, November and December, and in three months the only contracts or talks that had taken place had been a result of our referrals. I sat in that restaurant and asked Kieran to justify it, why should I renew the contract, what had you actually done?

I told Kieran that day that they would need to up their game and secure us paid sponsorships, not only that but that it was essential they secured us giveaways from our current and future clients. They never did up their game. I made it perfectly clear how essential it all was to the project and what figures we were looking at and again I was met by reassurances:

"We are good at what we do."

"We have major clients interested and in discussions to get involved."

Looking back, it is clear to see that we were never their priority and it seems that the whole change of business CEO for them really impacted on their ability to deliver anything never mind tens of thousands of pounds in sponsorship.

Seriously, it got so bad with Slingshot that I was chasing them for the updates, I don't know why because there was never anything of meaning to catch up on. It seemed that through the whole time of working with us Slingshot, Jackie and then Kieran had other things on their minds.

First of all it was Jackie leaving, then Kieran had a full month off to go travelling, (nothing got done), and then they moved office from the Business Design Centre to Oxford Street, it was one thing after another with at no point any urgency or importance placed on gaining us sponsorship.

There is no way that we could have started all over again with a new sponsorship company, the amount of work involved in that alone would push us back. Instead we tried our hardest to apply the pressure, to tell them we weren't happy with results. It made absolutely no difference whatsoever.

One sponsorship that Slingshot did secure and bring to the table was Gay Times and we were delighted with this. If we gave Gay Times £5,000 in advertising and brand exposure, they would in turn write a feature article about the exhibition, send out multiple online articles, invite their VIPs to the launch (promising us access to a whole host of LGBT VIPs) and loads more.

It wasn't cash in the bank for us, but we realised it's worth in potential to reach out to our target audience and being from a little village in Scotland and being scared of being gay to being featured in Gay Times Magazine was a pretty big deal for me.

We thought this was an amazing deal and if you went to the exhibition you would have seen Gay Times advertised all over the place. They are in the programmes, on all the billboards, on all our flyers, absolutely everywhere.

Part of Slingshot's contract is not only to gain sponsorships for the event but to manage those contracts and make sure both sides deliver what is contracted.

Where was our feature article in the magazine? Where was all the online coverage? Where were the LGBTQ celebrities? Given that we were never asked for any invitations we very much doubt any were ever invited.

There was an online post about the exhibition very early on but other than that absolutely nothing. Not only that but the Gay Times contact was Kieran's most guarded secret, so it wasn't as if we could contact them directly and push things along. The other problem with this contract is that Gay Times had exclusive LGBTQ rights to the exhibition and as such we were unable to secure other LGBTQ sponsors despite many being desperate to get involved. Well done Kieran, you really proved just how fucking hopeless you are with this.

It should have been an easy sell, an easy market to break into, instead you blocked one of the biggest publications from us and fucked it up royally.

To be honest with you I could write a couple of chapters in the book on how Slingshot managed to fuck up the whole financial side of it for us, but as I've said before, I try not to focus on the negatives in life all of the time. It is important to get our truth out there, to get our side of what went wrong out there as the one thing I can't bear the thought of is the girls themselves just thinking I was reckless or the Spice Girls' fans or the people supporting me thinking I was just winging it all along.

We had a sound business plan, a sound sponsorship package to offer and an amazing, relevant event. If I didn't have all of this in place it would have been impossible for me to get banks to believe in it and the finance companies.

The only way we were eventually able to bankroll the exhibition was because our business plan was so strong and the forecast for the first two years was realistically incredible.

It was an easy sell and people were jumping at it but Kieran the rugby-playing straight bloke couldn't close the deal and I know this from feedback I have had from various companies and partners.

Every time we struck up a new working partnership with any kind of company, I would introduce them to Kieran and tell them how they could get involved.

Not one became a sponsor, in fact so bad was Kieran

at negotiating that Andy from gass came straight back to me and told me how poor their conversation had been. Kieran hadn't even contacted him for weeks and when he did, he couldn't have been "less interested" I think were Andy's words. No negotiations, no get involved with this great event it could be amazing for your company, no sales pitch, nothing.

It wasn't that we ever gave up on Slingshot finding us sponsors, we were constantly sending them new intros for companies that had contacted us about being involved.

This was just one major aspect to the downfall of the exhibition. Had we managed to secure the sponsorships we were promised and lead to believe was possible then I truly believe the exhibition would still be running today and that we would still be welcoming Spice Girls' fans to the show now.

Even when we did manage to secure sponsorship from our own leads, they were managed by Slingshot and the money would either get eaten up by their costs or it would take weeks and months to filter through to us.

Meanwhile, we were continuing with the planning and we had a plan B to at least get the exhibition to a point where we could open to the public. After we were open, we were confident that we would be able to pay everything off with ticket revenues and merchandise sales.

Plan B involved a lot of bank loans and company loans in order to fund the different aspects of the exhibition that the sponsorships should have covered. We never once took out a loan that we were not confident of being able to pay back with the success of the exhibition.

Despite the lack of sponsorship, the whole exhibition vibe was incredible and the more we shared about it on social media, the more the interest seemed to grow.

We were gaining over one million impressions per month across our social media channels, it's not Victoria Beckham's following but it's a bloody good platform for a targeted audience, ideal for sponsorships and collaborations.

We had been told the numbers that we were achieving were fantastic, we had been told by Slingshot the coverage we were attracting was fantastic and everything we were doing should have been making life much much easier for them.

Instead I'm sure they managed to settle into their new office nicely. I'm sure Kieran enjoyed his vacations, long weekends, business trips away and everything else that distracted him from the job in hand. I'm sure Jackie Fast was somewhere sunning herself not giving one single fuck about the Spice Girls' Exhibition or its lack of sponsors.

When it came to the actually launch week and getting some items into the VIP gift bags or setting up information stands for what sponsors I had managed to secure for us, Kieran turned up. He turned up with boxes and boxes of junk, dumped them at the very entrance to the exhibition and then sat behind the front desk pretending to send emails and do some work.

He didn't make any attempt to set up the promotional stands of the sponsors or help out in any other way. I remember walking past him sitting at the front desk and not even being able to look at him properly, so disappointed was I with the outcome that I couldn't even hide how upset I was.

I think that was very evident as not one person from Slingshot was at the launch evening, I'm not even sure if they were invited to be honest and I really don't think I would have been happy to see them there.

No VIPs secured through them, no new leads on sponsorships, no significant gifts to give away to our VIP guests, no nothing. Complete fail.

People told me before I was writing the book that I might be liable to whatever... The thing is, everything in this book is the truth and my take on what happened.

I have offered companies the chance to respond to me and I have offered them the chance to give me an explanation of their failings.

If I had any explanations, I would be happy to share

them with you and put their side across. Instead all we have had is threats of slander, libel and threats of financial penalties.

When your failings in business have stripped someone else of every single asset they own, which is what has happened to me, why shouldn't that person be allowed to say what has happened to them.

Jackie Fast sent me a message on twitter shortly after I had messaged asking for my money back and asking if she could live with herself.

It reads:

> "If you are looking for headlines there are better ways to do so, if you are looking for a resolution there are better ways to do so. If you want to continue down this path I will be getting more involved as I do not take kindly to these kind of accusations."

> "I've since spoken to Slingshot and their legal team about what has transpired after my departure, your claims against what you think I said, evidence to the contrary and the general fact that it seems you are burning bridges everywhere you go. I will be taking legal action if this continues."

This is all following on from a tweet that I had sent Jackie asking for an answer as to why the sponsorship contract that she had initiated and in fact championed with her own reputation had failed so spectacularly.

I was met with the above threats of action, I was also met with accusations of slander and legal action for that as well and then swiftly blocked on social media.

Slander, Jackie, is given the following definition in the oxford dictionary:

> 'The action or crime of making a false spoken statement damaging to a person's reputation'
>
> Verb 'To make false and damaging statements about someone'

Feel free to point out what part of the above involving you is not true? I look forward to that day.

10

Welcome to Spiceworld – It's Crazy!

It really really really is a pretty mental thing to get caught up in and the press coverage had been building slowly and steadily like we had wanted. Then we hired Chuff Media (PR Company) and the Spice Girls had THAT meeting at Geri's house and boom! Suddenly overnight everyone wanted to speak to us about the exhibition and about the Spice Girls and what could possibly be coming up for them. It's a really surreal and strange thing to be thrust in to.

Phone calls asking if I could be in London first thing the next morning to do a live interview with someone, emails coming in asking if I could be in Manchester to be on BBC Breakfast news, but whilst I was there could I just do another three or four different interviews with different radio stations.

Everybody wanted to see a piece of the memorabilia whilst having a chat, so it was up to me drag my ass up and down the length of the country from one interview to the next carrying cases of clothes. Occasionally driving for hours, but most commonly from Liverpool to Media City in Manchester with a car full of mannequins, costumes, platform shoes and anything else Spice Girls.

One time I went to an interview at Media City in Glasgow for a BBC Scotland teatime show with a couple of presenters that I had grown up watching on the telly. It was the most bizarre thing ever going to the studio to rehearse in the afternoon (as it was a live show they wanted to set up the shots of the costumes) and bumping into all of these faces that I instantly recognised.

The studios themselves are housed in this gigantic building that is all completely purpose built and state of the art for filming. As you are walking through it to the studio you walk past all kinds of production meetings, filming segments and God knows what else. It was completely fascinating.

For the teatime programme they had asked me to bring along the centre stage star from Viva Forever, it was something a little more abstract, which besides the costume pieces would make an amazing talking point.

Neither me nor the producer had for one second thought about the security of it and when the security guards asked if I had anything in my bag, I had to boldly admit:

> "Yeah, sure, a giant oversized ninja-style star."

They just started laughing at me thinking I was joking but when I explained that I really did have a massive sharp metal star in my bag they were not very happy about it. I didn't get put in handcuffs or anything, but I was swiftly marched away from the main security area to a little side desk until they had confirmed that I had indeed been asked to bring it with me.

When they asked me if I had anything else to make them aware of, I was half tempted to make something up and see how they reacted but the good boy in me had a laugh with the security guards and kept my sarcasm to myself.

I took my babysitter from when I was a little boy, Alison, with me to the studios for the actual recording. I was a little nervous and despite being the most anxious person in the world Alison has a calming and comforting influence on me. She has been around since I was a little boy and is one of my best friends now and a cherished family friend. I grew up with Alison and she always has an ability of looking me in the eye and telling me to go for it or to reassure me that everything will be okay.

I thought Alison would enjoy the experience, she was like a little school kid all giddy and looking around at everything. I suppose I had been the same just a little earlier in the day. She of course laughed at me getting make up on and laughed when I tripped over something, keeping me grounded. Whilst I was so excited, it was a pretty big deal being on the telly with presenters I grew up with, on a programme I was familiar with, and going out live to my home country for the first time ever.

It was a great buzz, and it wasn't until we were already back outside the building after the filming when the presenter caught up with us in the car park to let us know that Geri was in the studios filming an episode of Mrs Browns Boys. Oh no, we were gutted to have missed her and there was no way we were getting that bloody ninja star back through security to get back in. Damn!

As a rule, I do not stalk Spice Girls or indeed anyone else for that matter. I don't necessarily disagree with fans going and waiting for them at venues or occasionally at a stretch at their houses, but it is not my style. I kind of understand if you have travelled all the way from Canada or somewhere and you are hoping to catch a glimpse of your icon, but to stand outside their houses or places of work has never been my thing and doesn't always sit easy with me. The only time I have met any of the girls is either by sheer chance, at a signing event or at a public event they are hosting. So, it was a real shame to miss Geri at the BBC in Scotland, I had her trainers and one of her costumes with me as well.

There were so many interviews with different people and for different channels and magazines that it does become a little bit of a blur at times and it did take over from some of the work I was meant to be doing on the actual exhibition itself.

The first big TV interview I had was for BBC Breakfast and the presenters were just a bit snide about the whole thing, especially the guy. I can't remember his name, smarmy Jackson or something I am sure. He waited until the end of the interview to throw in the question:

> "So, they all must be a bit skint, are they just in it for the money?"

What an absolute arsehole you are mate, trying to sensationalise my interview with you for a cheap shot at a tabloid headline? The other presenter could see that I wasn't happy, and I can't remember really what my response was, something along the lines of...

> "I don't think any of them are particularly skint, but I wouldn't claim to know what's in their bank accounts and wouldn't ask you what's in yours."

He apologised on air as it was pretty obvious, I was peeved with him and he did try to apologise after as well, but I didn't give him much of a chance. I knew exactly what he'd tried to do and unfortunately for him it didn't really work.

What it did do for me was prove that I could handle myself on the spot in an interview and not only that, the Spice Girls' fans who had seen it were happy with my response and happy that I was able to defend the girls a little. I got some nice messages of support that day from other fans and it made me enjoy the press for what it was after that.

Over the next few months the press interviews would get more frequent and again started taking me away from the project more than I wanted it to. Here I was getting more press than we could ever had imagined but it was causing us other problems.

The St Pancras Hotel at Kings Cross became like a second home for a few months and I still have regular contact with them now. The grand staircase was the location for filming 'Wannabe', the Spice Girls' first music video, but it is also now one of the most Instagrammable staircases in the world. It is so grand and fantastic that it makes the perfect backdrop for any interview relating to the Spice Girls and everyone from Vogue Magazine to Rolling Stone and the American News channels wanted to film there.

We had also done a little bit of filming there ourselves for some promotional videos for the exhibition, some of which I have yet to see the footage. Must be on an editing room floor somewhere but again there is more coming up about that soon…

Press and interviews became a part of daily life and the more we did of them the more routine they became and the less exciting they became. Occasionally you would go to one and it would be Fizz from Corrie or someone equally cool but other than that it was mostly the same questions over and over again just in a different location.

"How long have you been collecting?"

"How much money have you spent?"

"What is it about the Spice Girls?"

"What is your most expensive item?"

"What is your favourite piece?"

And of course:

"Who is your favourite Spice Girl?"

One other thing about all the press interviews is that everything is always rushed, with the exception of the Australian Morning TV channel who booked three months in advance, everything was literally a phone call and:

"Can you be here in the morning?"

Or

"Will you be free at 11.30pm this evening to do an interview with radio?"

And so on.

None of it was ever a chore for me. I could talk about Spice Girls all day long and not get bored. There are days with the exhibition where I did talk about Spice Girls all day long and I was in my absolute element.

The closer we got to the launch of the exhibition, the bigger the interviews seemed to be getting. First, we had started with a few interviews surrounding the

Spice Girls and then some local radio shows about the collection and about the upcoming exhibition.

With Chuff involved it migrated to full blown photo shoots with Vogue and cars picking us up to go to ITV at 4.30am.

The best interview that we had without doubt was with the Lorraine Kelly show at ITV studios. It was a few days before the launch of the exhibition and the Spice Bus had come to London for the interview. The interview itself was with Dan Wootton and I'd read his column and watched his gossip chats for years. He was always a champion of a Spice Girls' Reunion.

It was a stunning morning with not a cloud in the sky. Alex and I got picked up at my house at 5am by a car to take us to the ITV studios. We hadn't gotten to bed until late the night before and the week so far had been crazy with building the exhibition and other interviews.

Alex and I giggled in the back of the car on the way to the studios. It was a proper treat and I think we both took a moment to sit back and take in the experience. Chauffeur driven on the way to the Lorraine Kelly show to do an interview about an exhibition that I had planned and created from the start. The interview was going to be on the actual Spice Bus that we had worked hard to have fixed up (more about that later) and we had some of the most iconic Spice Girls' costumes in the world to show off and talk about.

Sitting in the cab with Alex I mentioned that Mel B was going to be at ITV today because she was guest hosting on Loose Women. We were both so excited about the prospect that we might bump into her but knew that in reality Loose Women was on a lot later than Lorraine and we would probably be long gone by the time Melanie arrived.

When we arrived at the studio, we had to set up posters and mannequins on the bus so that it looked a bit better than the stage it was at. The mannequins for the costumes just managed to fit under the roof and no more, but what we didn't factor in was that the bus had to move with the mannequins on it. Cue Alex and I riding on the Spice Bus going into ITV studios in Central London.

Riding on that bus even for the short distance from the holding building around to the entry of the studios along about 300 metres of main road in London, was beyond doubt one of the highlights of the whole thing.

We were squealing with delight, both of us and even Steve the bus driver was having great fun. The traffic was crazy and London was mobbed with commuters travelling to work.

The reaction from people made the whole experience even funnier, literally rubbing their eyes in disbelief that the Spice Bus was on the road with two nobodies on the front of it waving like mad and laughing hysterically.

Steve got in on the action by beeping the horn every two minutes making people turn around and take even more notice. Beep beep, here comes the Spice Bus.

It was strange seeing people instantly grab for their phones to take a picture, grab their friends and point out the bus was there, or actually breaking in to dancing and singing routines at the side of the street.

It had been a mental rush trying to get the mannequins set up on the bus along with the posters, the dolls and a few other bits and bobs. It was roasting hot and the two of us were absolutely dripping but that bus ride made every single second of it worth it.

Twice in one morning Alex and I had looked at each other as if the whole thing was a dream. Months and months of work and we were having the time of our lives, still working our asses off and on no sleep, but it is moments like this that we will remember forever. Twice in one morning life seemed surreal and it wasn't even 8am yet.

With the Spice Bus parked up just outside the back entrance of the television studios it wasn't long until cars started turning up and dropping presenters off. First it was Ruth Langford who gave us a little wave and next it was Eamon Holmes. They turned up in separate cars about 10 maybe 15 minutes after one another.

Eamon was a real treat, again someone else who I'd

grown up watching on the television, what a gentleman he was. He went and put his bags down at the side of the road and came over for a chat with us.

"Oh wow, what are you doing here?"

Followed by:

"Oh, doesn't that sound marvellous, well done you!"

Eamon Holmes stayed and chatted with us for a couple of minutes about what we were doing there and then wished us all the best of luck with it. He stood happily and took pictures in front of the bus with us and with the people that were with us. What a gentleman.

In between all the chat with the editors and listening to what was going to be happening and where, then getting mic'd up and talking a little bit with Christine Lampard in the studio (Lorraine was on holiday) was all very surreal and just when I thought I was playing it cool and getting into it all. I looked out the front window of the bus to see Mel B arriving in a silver Mercedes.

I always try and keep myself calm when I am about to meet a Spice Girl because there has maybe been one or two incidents in the past where I may or may not have been a total twat in their company. There may have been one day in Glasgow with Mel B where I just walked up to her and spluttered:

"Yipppppeeeee!"

In my own head it made sense, it was from the start of her own single "Feel so Good" and I meant to say something like I loved that single and that initial yippee at the start but instead I walked straight up looked her in the eye and simply said "Yippeeee!" What a twat!

As I walked up to where the car had stopped outside the studio door, I could feel my heart absolutely racing and had I no idea what I was going to say to Scary Spice who was RIGHT IN FRONT OF ME!!

"Good morning Melanie."

I don't think I could have sounded any chirpier or camper if I had tried.

"Good morning, how are ya?"

Was Melanie's reply but to be honest I was a little taken aback. It was a raspy gruff good morning, and before I could bite my tongue:

"Oh dear Melanie are you ok? Have you hurt your throat?"

After coughing and clearing her throat Melanie quickly came back with:

"No, you cheeky bugger, I've just woken up and was out late last night, what's that doing here?"

Melanie was pointing to the Spice Bus and kind of smiling. I really wasn't sure if I'd just majorly pissed her off, but she seemed in good spirits.

> "Right I'm off to get my morning coffee and get some make up on and then I'll be back out for a chat."

Melanie ran off into the studios quickly and I couldn't believe that I had just had a brief chat with the one and only Scary Spice. I didn't for one second think that Melanie was going to pop back out to see us so turned my attention back to the interview with Dan Wootton.

Dan Wootton, who was meant to be here half an hour ago and who still hadn't turned up.

He did eventually turn up and when he did, he couldn't have been any nicer to us. I loved Dan. I didn't always agree with what he had to say about things, but he was always so cheery and smiley that it was infectious.

In real life Dan is over the top infectious and smiley but he was also a bit of a stressor that morning. I'm sure he just wanted to get everything right, but I do remember at one point telling him to calm down a little and that everything would be absolutely fine.

Everything wasn't fine and to be honest anything that could have gone wrong with the live interview did go wrong.

After asking him so many times not to, Dan filmed a segment with one of Geri's robes where he literally scrunched it up in his sweaty hands and flung it from one side to the next, my heart was in my mouth the whole time and he could tell I was desperate to get it back off him.

We had lots of fun filming the little lead in segments, Dan on the driver's seat, Dan outside, Dan with the costumes, Dan holding the shoes, it really was amazing fun and an amazing experience to be having.

As it went to the live feed, I tried to reassure him again as he was trying to remember all the things to get into the slot.

> "Don't worry Dan, I know you love the Spice Girls, so if anything goes wrong, we can just have a bit of a chat about them and blag it."

The next thing I know Mel B has jumped on the bus with us:

> "You need to switch that camera off for a minute, stop filming."

As she pushed past the cameraman and headed straight towards me:

> "Right I've got a minute now, sorry about earlier, tell me all about what you're doing with it all."

We had a great little chat for a minute and Melanie went through all the costumes that were around us. She chatted briefly about all the memories the costumes were bringing back to her and how amazing it was to be back on the Spice Bus. There was a quick mention of the exhibition, which she wished us luck with and told us she knew all about it.

Melanie was tiny. I had known this from previous times we had met but this time she just had a pair of trainers on and a cap and so she really was very petite standing next to me. She kept holding on to me and hugging me and asking if it was okay to film on her phone a little bit and asking people to take pictures and film of us together. She literally grabbed a hold of my waist, pulled me as close to her as possible and pointed to the camera to get our pictures taken. Not only was Scary Spice beside me, she was pulling me closer for a photograph on her own phone, it wasn't a case of scary fan moment or 'please can I have a selfie', she wanted to film and take pictures for her own phone and for her own social media accounts.

The next thing I know my phone is going crazy with messages and Melanie has posed our picture on the bus on her Instagram account. Not only had I got to have a little chat Melanie had shared our picture to the world with a caption of the bus and the exhibition. Wow just wow.

It was all a total whirlwind of fun and laughing in true Scary Spice style. Melanie was so kind with her words and with taking the time to speak to me but before I knew it the producers were all shouting and getting their knickers in a twist. The next thing Melanie was gone and shouting good luck with the exhibition and…

3,2,1, and we are live on ITV on the Lorraine Kelly bloody show and right there and then my normal nerves of steel with interviews went out the window. My whole stomach flipped, and I don't even think I heard the actual question Dan had asked me. I knew what it should have been so answered that on auto pilot.

As the interview continued though we could see that things were not going to go as well as we had hoped. Dan banged his head on the bus a little and I tripped over one of the lighting men. I remembered where we needed to stand for lighting and sound and Dan was away out in the middle of the dark yonderness ha, he had completely forgotten the lighting instructions.

We continued our chat and went back and forth to the studio chatting with Christine and involving her with all of the glitz and glamour on the actual Spice Bus. The questions had been rehearsed a little but everything else that happened hadn't.

First thing was Dan lost the feed to the editor and couldn't hear the pointers he was getting. We ended up missing half of the segment out and instead had a really friendly and excited mates' chat.

The bus by this point was about 100 degrees inside. It was a roasting hot summer morning in mid London, the bus was compact inside and was always hot but the minute you added all the studio lights, the cameramen, the lighting men, me and Dan into the mix and it became an oven.

So, there we were at 8.15am on GMTV with sweat absolutely pissing off us both, Dan no feed in his ear, missing half the questions out and then all of a sudden, the lights start to go out and a poster falls off the wall in the background. It was like a sketch from the Ant & Dec show and I wasn't sure if they were going to jump out and surprise us at some point.

I'm sure it was all down to the heat but by the time we wrapped up the interview Dan and I were in absolute hysterics about it all. Bloody hell, anything that could have gone wrong during the live interview, did go wrong. Nevertheless, there was Dan Wootton and I standing on the Spice Bus going live to the nation having the time of our lives playing with and talking about some of the most iconic Spice Girls' costumes ever. It really was a pretty memorable experience.

As soon as the interview was finished it all de-rigs very quickly as with any interview, the mics are taken away, the cameraman disappears and that's it pretty much all over. This time was a little different.

Dan hung around for a few minutes to have a chat with us and generally be nice to me about everything and thanked me for reassuring him and calming him down a little. Other producers were coming out to get pictures with the bus and then one of the producers came up to us to ask if we could hang around a little bit longer. Melanie wanted to come and do a bit more filming with the bus and we could wait in the main canteen until it was all done.

From one mental experience to another this whole morning was the craziest it has ever been with the media and with the total surreal environment of meeting face after face that you recognised from TV. The next thing we were sitting in the café having breakfast and tea with them, chatting to all sorts of people from Rick Astley to Love Island contestants and God knows who else.

We waited in the café area for about an hour, the whole time Melanie walking back and forwards past us giving us a little smile, or saying I'll see you soon. Ruth Langford stopped for a chat and then we were called back to the bus to do some more filming with Melanie.

This time Melanie stepped out in a figure hugging gorgeous sequined dress, make up all done, hair done, smelling incredible and absolutely full of life. Earlier we had the privilege of meeting Melanie but this time it was easy to see we were in the presence of Mel B, Scary Spice.

Full of business she marched up to the bus and started making suggestions about where to film and what she thought was a good idea. A quick run through and at the end of her intro Melanie went to step off the bus. Unfortunately, it is an old bus and the step down is huge, I've seen so many people falling off it and Melanie was to be no different in towering heels.

I was standing right outside the bus door and was able to catch Mel as she fell over. That was it I was now declared her official catcher, clinging on to me and laughing at herself she very politely asked:

> "Please will you stand there for the real take and catch me if I fall off these bloody heels?"

I don't actually know if I answered or not. If I did answer I have no idea what I actually said, but there I was after chatting to Melanie a couple of times, now her official catcher. It was my job to stand there and make sure that Mel B didn't fall flat on her arse straight into a brick wall. I don't think I have ever taken any job so seriously in all my life. OMG what if she had fallen and I missed her?

This wasn't my last dealing with TV filming or interviews with the media, not by a long shot, but it was easily up there as one of my favourites along with filming in St Pancras Hotel. They say never to meet your idols, but I've met Mel B a few times now and seen her at her best and worst but every single time I am mesmerised by her. There is that absolute star quality, the feeling that you are in the presence of someone who is actually pretty special. Love ya Melanie, crazy lady.

11

We Have Lift Off

By the time of the launch evening we had been working day and night for two weeks solid in preparation and Steven and I were beyond exhausted. It was smiles and politeness when needed but under it all we were paddling like crazy just to even make it all a possibility. Money was incredibly tight as everyone was insisting that things were paid up front or they would not be delivering the items and since we were relying heavily on door sales the cash flow at this point was already strained and the strain was telling on us both.

We had been so busy with everything from the actual building of the exhibition to all of the press, that we literally didn't have the time to go and get something to wear for the launch and truth be told we didn't have the cash flow either. Our bank accounts were completely empty and if it hadn't been for my mum going and spending £500 on suits for Steven and me, we would have turned up in denims and t-shirt. As it happens that would probably have been a better look as we both had to rush to Marks and Spencer at 5pm at night with the launch starting at 7pm. My mum had bought us the wrong sizes and it was a mad dash around the shop to get anything at all that fitted us. In the sweltering summer heat, everything seemed to take ten times as long and ten times the effort. We both ended up looking like 60-year old bank managers with absolutely no style whatsoever. It wasn't because we didn't want to dress up, we wanted nothing more than to have the best fun ever, but instead we were in firefighting mode dressed like bored accountants or worse.

The VIP launch evening was a mixture of our families, the collectors, celebrity guests and fans who had paid for the experience.

Outside we had set up fan spectating areas, we were really going for it and of course had invited all five Spice Girls to attend. We knew they were aware of it and on the day of course the usual rumours swirled about attendance. With the Spice Bus in situ looking spectacular, the fan areas set up either side of the red carpet and with press starting to arrive, we were beyond excited to begin the show.

The only issue was the most horrendous thunderstorm of the summer directly overhead for a full 90 minutes before the red carpet was due to kick off. Fans outside were getting soaked, the Fixation theatre dance troop (I'll mention again in a minute) had to rehearse in the rain and at one point the sound cut out. These little superstars sang the songs themselves and continued to work through and rehearse their spectacular routine.

The spectacular multicoloured butterfly stilt walkers had to be delayed due to the weather and were only ever able to appear for a very short period of time. The music was sporadic and had to be lowered due to live press feeds from the red carpet. All of which really dampened the experience I wanted to create for everyone outside and entering into the exhibition. It was meant to be utterly spectacular and whilst we achieved everything we set out to with the performers it was a credit to them that they kept going at all. They did well to create the spectacular atmosphere in such challenging conditions.

Fixation theatre is one of those strokes of fate in life that somehow sneaks its way up on you. When we lived in Cyprus, I had helped in an amateur theatre on the military base we lived on. The theatre is where I got to know my little pink best friend, Nand. I developed a love of the theatre again and one day Pauline Bunton (Emma's mum) retweeted a picture of an old theatre company raising money for a project. It captured my attention and I pledged a little bit to their Crowdfunder appeal. I then went on to the Twitter account and read a little bit more. That's when I had the idea of contacting them and asking them to somehow be a part of the launch evening with a dance performance. The lady who runs the company is called Laura and we picked up a chat and arranged for a dance troupe to come and do a performance on the red carpet in front of the fans outside and to help raise the profile of what she was trying to achieve.

The first time I met Laura in person was the day before the launch evening and she came storming into the exhibition with a smile on her face, marched straight up to me, shook my hand and introduced herself. We had a walk around the exhibition so that I could show her where she could place promotional material within the exhibition. It was always my intention to support as many charities and good causes as possible with the exhibition and one of the ways of doing this is displaying information to raise awareness. It was on the walk around the exhibition that Laura blurted out:

"You do know I am Emma's cousin?"

Eh? What? Are you even for real? My jaw most probably hit the floor. I had absolutely no idea whatsoever, here was a dance troupe I had invited along because of a tweet and I was casually having a chat with Emma's family. Laura was obviously used to the reaction and couldn't have been nicer. Of course, I tried to play it cool, but I am sure she could see right through that.

As we walked around the exhibition I began to fill with dread. Emma is easily the hardest Spice Girl to collect costume pieces for. She has previously stated that she treasures it too much to give it away (totally understandable), but here I am taking a member of the Bunton family around a half finished exhibition beginning to explain why there are not as many

Emma items on show but also realising we were coming up to the Emma Bunton solo stage. The only stage in the exhibition not to showcase any solo costumes I found myself sweating at having to explain this. 'Emma likes to keep all her history safe', 'none of the collectors involved have any solo costumes', I could see Laura smiling as she started to tease me about it a little whilst telling me about all of the Emma shoes and costumes that she has been given. Yeah whatever Laura haha.

It turned out that Laura is an absolute scream and after the initial launch in the exhibition we had a great laugh drinking cocktails and champagne in the Hilton Hotel. Laura was the one trying to drag me out to the nightclub at 2am and I am beyond gutted that I had to decline due to opening the exhibition in the morning. I could have been out partying with a legendary Bunton and drunk calling Baby Spice at 3am. Only kidding that's totally not my style, it would have been Facetime or nothing ha. Laura, I take that rain check on that night out.

Back to the launch -

Without doubt the weather affected the numbers who turned out, but we were lucky really as even with the storms the space was tight around the bus and the hotel and two deep at the side of the carpet. We couldn't quite believe the turn out in the weather. We could maybe have got away with one side of crowd barriers, but people would have been a lot more crammed. Crowd barriers that cost us a whopping £5,000 are just one example of an unexpected expense that was added on last minute. Not exactly pennies and without it we were threatened with closure before we had even opened. The security around the event was phenomenal and for the launch evening alone was staggering.

With the best summer on record we picked the only day for months where there was a thunderstorm and torrential rain. The performers were amazing, but we lost a mega crowd outside because of the weather.

As it approached 6pm, we had to leave the exhibition where it was and admit that we maybe didn't have it as polished as we would have liked for the launch evening, but it would be ready for the opening the next morning and it was 98% complete.

Steven and I had to dart off to Marks and Spencer, change the suits and then dart back to the hotel to try and get ready in as little time as we possibly could. We were meant to be meeting our families and invited guests in the hotel bar for a drink before travelling on the open top bus to the red carpet. That was a bit of a disaster as well (more on Big Bus in a minute).

Poor Josh (man-child) was left to deal with everything at the venue as we had to slope off to get ready. He had to deal with all the catering, finalising all of the event, telling the camera crew and Ashley James (our gorgeous host for the evening) where to set up, sorting out Ashley's rider, which changed last minute as she wasn't feeling very well.

Back at the hotel it was a little different from the launch evening of the Cyprus exhibition. I'd had my thyroid removed and medication for my stomach ulcers was helping loads. I didn't throw up once whilst getting ready or whilst at the launch evening, which in itself is a total bonus.

Putting on the suits and ties we both knew this was not how we wanted to be dressed for the evening and my hair as usual for any event was a complete washout nightmare.

I'm fast approaching 40 years old but as a little barber who cut my hair a couple of months ago was happy to point out:

"You don't dress 40."

And I don't. I don't walk about with Marks and Spencer's slacks on or trousers. I like to wear jeans and converse and a t-shirt. I hate being nearly 40 so there is no way I am going to dress like I am. I do also realise my limitations and do not dress like I am 19.

The suits didn't cut it for us but what could we do now and at least I had a pink tie to represent my little Nand. We gave each other a kiss, I'm sure Steven gave me a bit of a pep talk, but I have no idea what he said to me and then we were off.

Holding hands walking down the hallway on the way to the biggest night of our lives. Months and years of work had gone into this and this was the moment we got to showcase it to the world. With Steven by my side and cheering me on I'd happily take on the world. Head held high it was time to get the party started. It didn't matter that I had butterflies or that my brain was not working properly, I had Steven, holding my hand and telling me to go for it.

Bing, the lift doors open to a whole host of our friends and family all dressed up in their finest looking beyond incredible. Jennifer (my bestie forever) was there, my mum, Alison, Stevie C, Ruby, Max, Christine (my best boss ever and now lifelong friend), Steven's sisters and so many more people.

It was the best feeling in the world seeing everyone all happy, chatting away, drinking champagne and getting in the mood for the launch evening.

Outside the hotel there were fans from all over the world all around the barriers, the butterfly stilt walkers were doing their thing, Fixation Theatre had already performed and absolutely knocked it out of the park for us, the sun was starting to shine and the carnival atmosphere that I wanted to create was starting to build.

Time for a very quick drink with everyone to watch the entertainment that was going on and to make sure everyone was there that needed to be and it was off round the back of the hotel and down a little alley, through the car park to the waiting open top double decker London Bus.

One of our working partners was the Big Bus Company in London, they were meant to be providing us with a Union Jack bus but instead had completely fucked up (more soon) but at least we had one of their buses with an open deck for everyone.

All of the guests on the bus, including my mum, grandad (Stevie C), Jennifer and the rest of our friends and family, were meant to travel just around the corner and get off the bus outside the Business Design Centre before us.

We were meant to arrive in a leopard print Taxi but that went a bit wrong and we ended up with just a normal black hackney, at least it was in keeping with the Olympics theme and how the girls arrived for the launch night of Viva Forever.

Even though we waited for ten minutes after the bus had left, to allow time for everyone to get inside, the bus had gone the wrong way and ended up on a one-way street doing half a tour of London.

Steven and I got there before the bus anyway and to be honest it worked out well. It was actually nice to be there to see it coming around the corner with all my nearest and dearest on it.

Walking up that red carpet was the most bonkers thing in the world ever! I went straight over to people waiting outside to speak to them. I felt so guilty they had been standing in the rain and was keeping my fingers crossed for them that a Spice Girl might turn up, wouldn't that be nice.

We had gassProductions streaming to our Twitter feed live from the red carpet with Ashley James presenting it. She looked absolutely stunning in a striking hot pink dress and heels.

It's all a little bit of a blur, after talking to the people outside I don't really remember the details of much else. I remember Andy from gass telling me to smile whilst Ashley was asking me questions, but I have no idea what Ashley had asked me.

I remember standing there chatting away thinking to myself 'I hope I actually answered the question she asked me'. I was totally star struck, I did love Ashley and was a fan, but she was reassuring more than anything. The one thing I will say is that she is beyond beautiful! Her skin, her hair, her body and most of all her eyes, are incredible.

Ashley was also our DJ for the party inside as well, so once she had got all of the introductions sorted outside for the live stream she was upstairs in no time running the music for us.

Steven and I posed for the press on the first landing, this is something I could do all day every day and felt like a true superstar at this moment. The press were moved to the first landing inside as it had been raining and stormy and they didn't want to get soaked. It worked as a press call, but it meant that nobody was standing outside for fans. They were told I was the organiser by our PR company and all of a sudden there was about 30 flashing light bulbs going off, really strong flashes that make it incredibly hard not to squint.

Of course, I stood there and grinned like a Cheshire cat thinking I was actually playing it cool. Girl Power pose, shift weight to alternative leg, thank all the press for coming to cover the event, peace sign and that was it. Time to go and join our guests and let the fun begin. I think I hid the fact that I was absolutely shitting myself and shaking all over quite well.

As we walked up the final flight of stairs I was nervous. I had been a little nervous for the red carpet, arriving and for the interview with Ashley, but right now right here as we were about to turn the corner to see if there was actually anyone there. This is when I was most nervous, would anyone actually be there or would it be a repeat of the Cyprus launch, fun, but a bit of a wash out.

With rain and thunderstorm on top I really was half expecting to turn the corner and see it empty.

Exactly the opposite happened. I turned the corner and the place was absolutely buzzing! It was full of people I recognised but not only that, everyone looked so bloody glamorous and amazing. The music was playing at a low level and everyone was mingling perfectly.

Not everyone in the room knew each other and I

can't claim that I knew everyone either. What I was delighted with was, here I am having this really surreal moment of my life and when I look around, I can see faces of people that I absolutely adore mixing with celebrities and having great fun.

The crowd was beyond amazing and I had structured the evening so that everyone would gather at the beginning to have Spice Girls' themed cocktails and snacks whilst waiting to be allowed the first peek of the finished exhibition.

Everyone was so excited and talking about the Spice Girls, of course Spice Girls' songs were playing and everyone from the costume designers, some of the cast of Viva Forever, reporters from Vogue magazine and of course the celebrities like Atomic Kitten's Liz McClarnon (who was so lovely), some of the stars of Love Island and loads more, were having a great evening.

Chizzy Akudolu who plays Mo Effanga in Holby City, and who is one of Steven's favourite actresses, was on a mad dash to another event and asked for a quick sneak preview of the exhibition. I found myself taking ten minutes out to show her around the exhibition quickly before she had to shoot off. Chizzy vowed to come back and sent some lovely messages of support on social media. A real crazy highlight for me of the launch evening.

It also gave me the chance to stand back and take a look at what was going on around me. The flowers for my mum, Alex and a few others had arrived so as I was looking at them, I was being briefed about what was next. In that moment I was able to look around at everyone in their jewels and their best dresses, smiling, dancing and having a great time. Perfect.

A tap on the shoulder from Josh, it was 8pm and it was time to get the speeches over with and allow people to go have a viewing of the exhibition. Honestly Josh is the one that kept the whole VIP night flowing, he's a good boy most of the time and really pulled it out of the bag for us that night.

Taking the microphone from Ashley James, I gave a quick five-minute speech. I can't really remember what was said and whilst I was a bit nervous chatting, I remember being more euphoric than anything else. Everything had been leading up to this moment and so far, we were smashing it.

I declared the exhibition officially open and handed the mic over to the one and only Conleth Kane. Conleth had covered Melanie C's 'I Turn To You' and it is stunning. He also has an amazing song that he wrote himself called 'Proud'. I don't normally feel the need to crusade about being a gay man, but this song is subtle, smooth and gorgeous and sums up a coming of age perfectly.

Conleth sang his heart out for us (thanks buddy) and then it was back over to Ashley to play her set and keep the party going whilst people dipped in and out of the exhibition.

It was now that I would get the real first reaction to the exhibition.

All the collectors involved were there, so it was a real group affair for all of us and I really hope I managed to make the other collectors proud of what I had achieved and put together. It certainly wouldn't have been the incredible size it was without their costumes involved.

Six collectors in total all with varying amounts of input into the project but all equally as passionate about one thing, the Spice Girls. It was our passion for these amazing ladies that set us apart from other people but gave us something very unique and quirky in common.

Jyle from Australia, Andrea from Italy, David from France, Samuel from Germany, Liz from Manchester and me from Scotland, it really was a collection of collectors from all over the Spiceworld.

We were also incredibly lucky to have some of the original costume designers involved. Dane 3001, Adrian Gwillym from Academy Costumes and Dee Izmail. The guys are amazing and easy to get on with, but Dee and I did have a few differences of opinion regarding the costumes and standards for the exhibition.

The reaction to the exhibition and the costumes on display was beyond incredible, and with every person I spoke to I became prouder and prouder of our achievements.

What was a real thrill for me was seeing how amazing it looked full of people, people who were all having a great time with either champagne or Spice Girls' cocktails, taking selfies, dancing along to the background music, being silly, reminiscing with 'remember whens' and 'oo I had that'. It was exactly how I had wanted it to be.

Radio presenters, celebrities from all walks of life, reporters, press and social media influencers were all there having a great time but most importantly they were all tweeting amazing photos of it out to their followers.

Gaby Allen from Love Island and then later Big Brother, put out a picture of herself on the staircase leading up to the exhibition. Legs wide open in a proper 'Girl Power' pose with the words 'Spice it Up' in between her legs. It is still one of my favourite pics from the whole exhibition. It's Girl Power at its best.

The whole time in the venue was then spent chatting with people and generally mingling and taking selfies. I must admit it was bloody awesome fun.

Every so often I would bump into Steven and we'd smile or catch a quick chat about something and then we would be off on our separate directions mingling again. We have never felt the need to hang off each other on a night out or at an event and in fact we have begun to use it as a strength. We were able to split up on the same mission, spread the word and double the charm offensive.

It's hard to sum up what it meant to me to get the reaction we were getting to the exhibition and to see everyone not only there but having a really great time. I definitely had a few private teary-eyed moments.

Before I knew it, the Business Design Centre staff were approaching us and telling us that it was time to move all of the guests out. One strict rule the venue always had was, everyone must be out of the building by 10pm. It was for this reason that we had arranged to continue the after-show party at the Hilton Hotel which was literally 20 steps away for everyone.

I couldn't believe that was the time and that the months of planning and organising the launch evening was now over and done with. I had a quick walk round and check of the exhibition and then trusted the staff to do their thing locking up before making my way to the after-show party.

12

If You Can't Dance

The Hilton Hotel in Angel Islington is one of the most amazing hotels I have ever had the pleasure of working with and there is nothing that I can write in a book than can do justice to the level of service they gave to us that evening. Not just that evening but right from the beginning and even up until now, where, unfortunately Spice Girls' Exhibition Ltd were never able to pay them in full. The Hilton Hotel and the team there have handled themselves with style, dignity and the best manners I have seen in the hospitality business.

Richard Jackson and his team had arranged so many nice little surprises for us and looked after our guests so incredibly well that night.

First, all of the staff had t-shirts on that had our logo and #SpiceUpLondon on them, we didn't know about it, so it was a lovely little touch and surprise for us when we walked in.

They had two big burly and rather handsome security men standing at the front door and the whole bar area was closed off for us. They had also managed to place our roll up banners in exactly the right place in order to create amazing photo opportunities and back drops for us.

Normally I would say what happens at an after-show party stays at an after-show party but there are a few little things we really should mention.

The champagne and cocktails were free flowing, and everyone was in great spirits, chatting away to each other having a great time.

We had arranged for two of the boys to play a live acoustic set, by two of the boys I mean Josh's friends Seth and Harry who had been there all week helping us to set up the exhibition. The boys between them, built all of the information stands and rope posts. The set they played was amazing and included some covers of Spice Girls' songs of course. The boys are budding musicians and actors, so I think they were in their element performing to all sorts of people. They had got the set perfect for us and it really was the perfect background music for the night.

There were no major dramas on the evening but there was one point that was actually funnier than drama. Two of the guests who I couldn't remember the names of even if I wanted to, started a little spat. One was a guy from a radio station, and one was a guy who had bid on a ticket. Both were equally as gay and outrageous as each other and rather than punches thrown it literally was a lit bit of pushing and hissing.

It was so funny to watch these two grown boys actually hiss at each other that the security guards were actually chuckling as they split it up. I went over to see what was going on and both boys were equally as drunk as each other. It turns out some people can't handle all five Spice Girls' cocktails with champagne on the side.

There may have been some fornication of some kind, but I would never be at liberty to discuss that. There was a peacock that walked out of the hotel the next morning that I wasn't too happy about and quickly tore the feathers off. Don't mix business with pleasure, number one rule and when it could have had an effect on my business, I wasn't best amused.

Two little chappies who made an unannounced appearance at the party were our two little rescue beagle-type doggies, Benji and Junior. Having not long moved to London we didn't have anyone to look after them and the hotel allowed pets.

Our boys are demons with other dogs but with humans they absolutely love being the centre of attention. We only went to let them out for a pee and all of a sudden, they were the stars of the show for five minutes. Running around outside the Spice Bus, approaching everyone they could including Liz

McClarnon and Paisley (from Tattoo Fixers) for cuddles and praise.

The funniest thing about the dogs was Junior in the elevator. We'd never had the dogs in a lift before and as with everything else Benji took it in his stride. Junior was fine going into the lift but the second it started going down he absolutely freaked out. With his legs wide apart and his claws scratching at the floor the sensation of falling must just have been too strange for him.

The problem then came when we were trying to get Junior back in the lift to go back up to the room. No way in the world was he getting back in that contraption and after trying everything from pushing and pulling to a treat there was only one thing for it. Pick him up like a baby. Bloody daft dog makes me laugh every day.

Despite the earlier thunderstorm the evening had turned out to be gorgeous and warm and so most of my evening was spent outside with the smokers and with my mum and friends who were all sitting just at the front table by the entrance.

It was an amazing surreal (again) setting that I had to take a moment to stand and realise and get a little bit emotional over. There I was with the Spice Bus in front of me, all lit up and looking incredible (I had arranged for that to be there, wow), everyone was chatting away and getting along. All the major Spice Collectors were there, my Mum, Stevie C, the Spice

Girls' costume designers and a whole host of celebrities and it was all for the opening of an exhibition that I had created.

No Spice Girls had turned up, which of course was a bit disappointing ultimately, but at the same time I had always known it was going to be a big ask. We did however have everything else that mattered, and we certainly made the most of the evening.

I'm not cutting the paragraph short, my memory genuinely becomes a little hazy at this point. I know the staff had offered or brought us snacks and made my mum something special and I know that even though I was sad the launch evening was over (for us anyway) I was so so happy to get to my bed and cuddle up with Steven. Every single bit of my body ached, but it was worth it.

The hotel room was really comfortable with a gorgeous huge balcony that looked out over the London skyline, that in itself was special but easily the best thing about the hotel room; the bed. The king size memory foam mattress that you sink into and seem to instantly fall into a coma-like sleep.

Lying there that night cuddled into the best man in the whole world, as tired as I was and as comfy as the bed was, my mind wasn't for switching off and my face hurt from smiling.

Me, Stevie C,
Steven and the
fabulous Nand at
our second
wedding in
Cyprus

My Absolute rock
throughout it all! They
say behind every great
man there is an even
greater lady, well here
she is. Alex the ball
breaker Maughan.

Georgia, crazy
lady. There
would have
been no
Manchester
without her.

The Girl Power lights at the entrance to #SpiceUpCyprus

The timeline stage at #SpiceUpCyprus and if you look carefully at the left hand side of the picture you can see the choir rehearsing for the VIP opening night.

The magical entrance staircase for #SpiceUp London

HEAR YOU
WHEN ME
AND MAKE THE
TO
SEE YOU'LL BE THERE
TOO MUCH
IS IT
TWO BECOME ONE
LET
WHO DO YOU THINK YOU ARE
YOU BETTER
MY LOVER
WANN BE
IF YOU

The gorgeous Max & Ruby (Nand's kids) with Nelly the elephant.

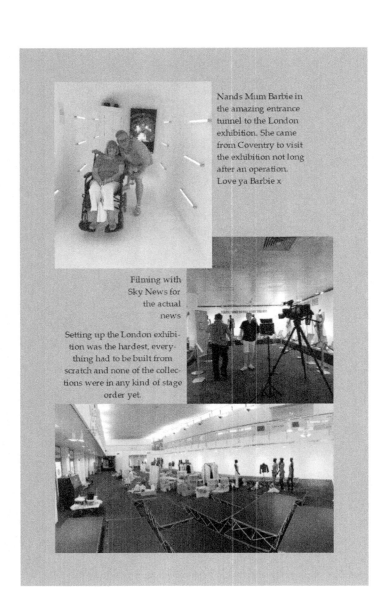

Nands Mum Barbie in the amazing entrance tunnel to the London exhibition. She came from Coventry to visit the exhibition not long after an operation. Love ya Barbie x

Filming with Sky News for the actual news

Setting up the London exhibition was the hardest, everything had to be built from scratch and none of the collections were in any kind of stage order yet.

Mel B on the Spice Bus at ITV studios, sheer chance meeting but so amazing. Melanie couldn't have been any nicer.

The Spice Bus in all her glory taking pride of place outside #SpiceUpLondon

Dan Wooton with one of Jyle's costumes outside the Spice Bus filming for ITV

Broken down Spice Bus being recovered from a motorway service station!

Natalie Halliwell on the Spice Bus, a huge highlight for me to get to have a chat and a laugh with Geri's sister.

Naughty Nic, Christine, My Mum & Allison, the morning after the launch evening, I think.

All the contributing collectors from around the world, Jyle, Liz, Samuel, David, Andrea & Me.

The Weekends in Manchester Central were amazing, the vibe was cool and much more relaxed in Manchester.

The Spice Girls bedroom. Everything in the room was Spice Girls. I still wish I had a house in my room like this!

Me, Steven and the two Alexes on our way into the VIP night of #SpiceUp Manchester

The two Spice mums on their visit to #SpiceUpManchester

Oliver (who opened Watford for us) in London, check out the phone cover.

The Manchester warehouse was my least favourite exhibition.
We made the best of what we had but I never got used to it.

The entrance to the Watford exhibition, with blue lighting to make it
look cold and winter wonderland themed. At the bottom left of the
picture you can see Emma's tour trunk gifted to me.

TV interview in London for Australian Morning TV. Getting set up at 12.30am

Alex Lodge (legend) spilling all the exhibition contents as he was walking them over to the second Manchester venue.

Alex & I on a mate date watching the incredibly Melanie C perform at Boisdale

The five Spice Girls Christmas trees at #SpiceUpWatford.

It's the 'Elephant in the room' my best friend, a gorgeous, ickle, pink, sparkly elephant. Of course it is Nelly the Elephant.

Steven and I at the launch of #SpiceUpLondon check our bank managers suits out.

Nand

13

Who Do You Think You Are?

I didn't mind the interviews, the cameras, playing to the producers and acting the crazy Spice fan. 'Spice Girls' Superfan' is a phrase I dislike a lot and always one I would try and steer journalists away from but always the one that gets used. I am a fan, I love the ladies, they taught me how to believe in myself. However, I know of bigger fans than me, people who live, breath and sleep Spice Girls. Fans who know every aspect of every concert and appearance, every dance move and every single line to every song, Spice Girls, Solo, unreleased and obscure.

I'm mostly a collector and a huge fan. As I say all the time, the girls taught me to believe in myself, not to be afraid to be different and to work hard to achieve my dreams. I love the music, I love the concerts and I love the costumes, but I don't study them all the time. I don't follow them around the country to signings all the time, to every appearance and I have never waited for them outside of work or at their homes. Whilst I like that they maybe know about the exhibition I would hate for them to think of me as some crazy stalker that always turns up like a bad penny.

Back to the launch weekend. It kind of ran away from us if I am honest. It was so manic trying to get the exhibition ready on time and with me being away from the venue most of the time or tied up with camera crews it really all fell down to the amazing team I had around me. Steven was running around with a phone to one ear and giving directions to people on the floor building things, whilst hammering in nails and stages at the same time. He also had to deal with all the technical side, the ticket scanners, the music, the movies, the performers, and the list goes on.

Josh, Steven and Alex managed it all well and had a team who they were able to direct. Surprisingly, after pissing us off a little by avoiding most of the heavy lifting (he has a habit of being found standing back with his hands on his hips watching others getting the back-breaking stuff done) Josh really stepped up to the plate. He was able to give directions to others on the wheres and hows and he was also the one who almost single-handedly made sure the VIP launch evening went ahead at all.

I was a little hungover, but at the same time I was absolutely buzzing from the excitement of it all. I looked like death on Sky News and of course it was the one interview that was played over and over again for the full opening day (not that I was complaining about the coverage). It must have been a slow news day as there was my hungover face twice an hour on Sky News around the world.

I had the easy job on the opening morning. I had to stand and smile and chat to Sky News, BBC News and a few others. After that I had to show a few VIP reporters around and before I knew it, it was time for my first guided tour of the exhibition.

Before we get to that there was one major issue we had to deal with, the Big Bus Company. What an absolute nightmare this company were to work with and I wish I had listened to my Nand when she told me to stick with what I was good at. The bus tours etc. were added fluff and I should stick to just the exhibition. If I had listened things could have been very different.

The Big Bus wankers had been contracted to provide us with a Union Jack covered open topped double decker bus. The design of it was incredible and had taken Alex and I around 20 hours all together to come up with and perfect. It was also a nice tribute to both the girls and Nand, with Nany Sparkle written on the front (Nand's Granny name).

Two days before the bus tours were due to begin (our opening day) we got an email from Big Bus wankers to say they were pulling out and would no longer be providing us with a bus at all. There were some issues with finances at this time so we hadn't paid them everything but even still we had paid them a lot, at least enough to cover the first two weeks of operation and we had also managed to get together the £6,000 to have the bus wrapped in a Union Jack design. So here they were 24 hours after we had paid them £6,000, pulling out of the deal altogether. We had sold hundreds of tickets for the bus tours and this was an absolute nightmare for us all.

I told Big Bus Company that I was on my way to their offices and that I demanded to see the Union Jack wrapped bus that we had paid for. They had told me on the phone that it had been done, so I demanded to go and see it. It wasn't long until they changed their minds.

As soon as I had said I was going down to see the bus we had paid for we got an email from them showing us that they had received a breach of copyright from another bus company in London who ran Union Jack bus tours. Not only that but they had raised this copyright infringement way back in February. Big Bus never had any intention of giving us a Union Jack bus. If they did, they knew they would be breaking copyright but instead of telling us and risking us going to their competitors they just said nothing. We could have announced that it wasn't a Union Jack beforehand, we could have made changes to the advertising, but instead they left it right to the last minute and there was nothing we could change.

With hundreds of people due to turn up over the opening weekend for the bus tour I had to make the decision that the tour had to go ahead without the Union Jack. People would be more disappointed if I cancelled the full tour rather than running it with a normal tour bus.

In hindsight it might have been better to cancel the tour and offer people the chance of afternoon tea or some merchandise, as it was a disaster from start to end.

They hadn't prepared any music for the bus. The script I had given them had never been shared with the guide. The guide was a straight bloke called Hamish who knew nothing about the Spice Girls, nice enough lad but just not right in any way for a Spice Girls' themed tour. He knew his stuff about London but not Spice Girls and blagging it with super fans who had booked the first weekend was not going to wash.

To top it all off, Hamish called a bus full of female Girl Power fans 'Birds' and then proceeded to crack open a can of beer halfway around the tour. Half of the bus thought he was funny and charismatic but a bit too much for the style of tour and the other half of the bus were furious.

I had been aware of the chaos before the tour had started. I had to give Hamish a quick run down and show him our book that might give him a few pointers. There were all sorts of Spice Girls' landmarks that should have been covered but instead Hamish chose to talk about Mel B's hard nipples in the Wannabe video. Massive fail!

Whilst the bus tour was proving to be a nightmare, the rest of the exhibition was actually running like a fairground. There had been queues outside before we opened, it was busy the way we wanted it to be and the reaction to the exhibition itself was incredible.

Both Guided Tours were sold out completely and I was beginning to get a bit nervous about the first one kicking off. With everything that had been going on with press and with the bus tour being a disaster from the start, it was 1pm and time for the first guided tour before I knew it.

As twenty people plus a few reporters lined up at the entrance of the exhibition, my heart was pounding. I had performed on stage loads both singing and acting and I suppose this wasn't so different. This time though I didn't have a script or lyrics and I was trusting my knowledge of the Spice Girls and the exhibition not to let me down.

There was nothing to worry about other than losing my voice. As soon as I had got those first two sentences out of my mouth, I was off and running, and I couldn't have been prouder showing off the exhibition and all of the costumes.

What we achieved from my vision and from my dream of creating the biggest music exhibition ever, was incredible. Hundreds of iconic Spice Girls' costumes, shoes and jewellery on display in a way that had never been seen before. Curated by me, designed by me but built so lovingly by so many people. I couldn't have made any of it happen without people encouraging me, without the support from people all over the world.

It wasn't hard for me to talk people around it. I couldn't have been prouder of it. The problem was stopping me talking. A tour that was meant to last between 60- 90 minutes had ran on to two and a half hours. 150 minutes of me rabbiting on about the Spice Girls and their costumes. Those poor people on that first tour, I'm sure it was maybe fun for about an hour.

By the time I finished that first guided tour I was on a total high and making my way down the stairs at the end, I was giddy about it, people were walking with me and still asking me questions about it, it felt amazing.

Little did I know I was walking into what felt like a bit of a warzone with poor Steven under attack on the front desk from lots of unhappy customers from the bus tour. We are so sorry to our customers we let down with the bus tour. It was not what we promised, and the Big Bus Company really didn't deliver what they were meant to, but ultimately the buck has to stop with me.

We promised refunds and freebies and some people were happy that we tried to make it right. In all of these situations though there is at least one person who is baying for blood and it doesn't matter what you say or do, they want to see a head or two roll for the fuck up. This is one part of customer service neither of us enjoys although Steven is a lot better at it and a lot more patient than I am. Steven to the rescue to sort out the refunds and anything else.

We worked hard with Big Bus wankers to try and get the tour right for the customers and to try and deliver what we had promised but ultimately it wasn't to be and they couldn't get it right.

We ended up having to refund over £15,000 worth of Big Bus tickets and with our already tight finances this became one of the nails in our coffin. It was definitely when we started struggling the most financially, money that was already paid out to people including the Big Bus Company, now had to be found to be refunded to customers and it wasn't pennies. The whole Big Bus debacle cost Spice Girls' Exhibition Ltd around £30,000 in total and had we continued to trade we would have looked into the possibility of taking them to court.

Anyway, putting Big Bus aside, the opening weekend was a huge success. The launch evening had been incredible and had been attended by loads of famous faces that were happy to tweet about it. The exhibition was crazy busy and both our book and merchandise were incredibly popular. The bus outside was a massive hit and the feedback we were getting was beyond incredible.

The guided tours were going amazingly well and

were easily my favourite part of the whole thing, telling people facts that they maybe didn't know about the costumes or about the Spice Girls themselves was amazing. To see people react and chat to their friends when I told them about 51 different flavours of Walkers crisps or 11 sets of official dolls or that the girls regularly swapped costumes. People were having fun and as a result everything was worth it.

We may have been crazy busy, running on empty and very little sleep but it was an incredible buzz. With the whole team around us all pulling together to get the job done under some very trying circumstances, I couldn't have been prouder of what we had achieved but also what we were continuing to do together. Everyone had their own strength and at this point it was heads down and get on with it. When you are leading a project like this, I couldn't have asked for more when the going was getting tough.

My whole team put their heads down and made me incredibly proud of them. They would maybe come up and ask me for a seal of approval but other than that they got on with every little bit and bob of the exhibition that needed to be fixed, polished or sorted.

My mum was still in London as were all of our guests, so we had arranged for them to go on the tour bus if they wanted or for them to have afternoon tea at the Hilton Hotel. The only problem was we couldn't join them for any of the fun. I think to be honest we wore them all out as by the Saturday night all was quiet on the family and friends front and we were beyond shattered ourselves.

We had decided to stay at the hotel for another night, not because we couldn't travel the hour home, but it was just much easier, and we still had a launch party to go to at Club De Fromage at the O2.

The exhibition closed at 8pm on a Saturday night, so Steven and I made our way back over to the hotel and were able to have a chat about what went well and what hadn't. We were both delighted with it, but the bus tour was a major concern. They had promised to get it sorted for us if we stuck with them and with hundreds more people booked on it, we had no choice.

Before we knew it, we were both out for the count sleeping in the hotel room. We had not set an alarm or anything and we could have slept through the public launch party. By luck I woke up at 12am with my phone beeping from a text message, it was our girl friends from Cyprus wondering where we were, they were at the O2 having a great night at the launch party.

"Shit, we've slept in!"

As I nearly nudged Steven off the bed.

Neither of us could believe that we were actually now going to have to drag ourselves out of bed, get ourselves ready and go clubbing. Now if you know

Steven and I this is not normally a problem for us, we maybe go home a little earlier than we used to, but we know how to have a wee party to ourselves.

This was extreme and both of us really struggled to get our acts together. We couldn't let the girls down though, they had travelled all the way from Cyprus for the launch and were now ready to party at our launch party.

We got to the O2 at around 1am and when we got there they refused to let us in, even after I explained it was the launch party for the exhibition, they still refused to believe us and we had to wait until the organiser got involved.

It turns out he was happy to have the party in our honour but wasn't expecting us to actually turn up and support the event. How crazy is that, a party in our honour and we weren't even expected to attend it. Worst of all we could have stayed in bed haha! Only joking of course.

It took us a while to get into it but to be honest if you have never been to one of the Club De Fromage evenings, I can't recommend it enough. The guy hosting it is amazing, the cheesy music, stage competitions and generally wall to wall madness is infectious.

Unfortunately, we couldn't stay for long, as much as we were starting to get into all the fun, we realised we had another full day ahead of us with the second day of the exhibition. It was due to be crazy busy again and so we did the sensible thing and bowed out early. Left the Cyprus girls to enjoy the cheesiness but I am sure they bowed out not too long after us.

Every part of my body ached as I got back into bed that night, but my brain was spinning. What an incredible couple of days it had been. Not everything was perfect but with events of this size it's very rare that absolutely everything runs smoothly. What we could be happy with, was every aspect that we were in direct control of had ran smoothly and was continuing to work well.

Time for some sleep hopefully, before having to do it all the next day and again for the next 26 days after that.

14

Holler

Not everything was perfect, but it was going well and there were some real highlights for us all to be proud of. The Spice Bus being there was a real privilege and proving hugely popular although that was a huge can of worms in itself (more later). The exhibition was popular despite a few grammar mistakes on the information displays and Melanie C's birthday month being wrong on one of the roll up banners.

Even by this point though money was very harsh and it was really starting to take its toll on us. We had a huge black hole from the sponsorship company to try and make up. We now had to refund thousands of pounds in bus tickets and the venue had slapped any extra additional charge that they could on to us.

With two weeks before the exhibition was due to open and with thousands of tickets already sold, the venue used this as leverage to be able to charge whatever they wanted on a couple of things.

First of all was the security costs. Two weeks before the event and after months of asking them for information we were told that the minimum number of security guards needed each day would be five and that it was our responsibility to pay for security at the front door, despite the fact the building always had security at the front door.

The security costs were phenomenal and an example of the venue not being up front with us. It's also important to mention that the venue were a little pissed off with us. They thought it would be a good idea to install a new escalator into the building at exactly the same time as we were running the exhibition. This meant dust, noise, disruption and all sorts of problems for us. After a lot of hard ball negotiations, we managed to get the venue to agree to do all the heavy work outside of exhibition hours, to block off the works with branded walls and to give us a discount on the venue hire. We managed to get almost £10,000 off the bill for the venue but I am 100% positive they found other ways of getting this discount back from us.

The security costs being one of them. Here we were on the final lead up to the exhibition with absolutely everything else in place and the venue send us a security bill of over £50,000 that they had never mentioned. Never once in any tours of the building did they mention a security man dedicated to sitting in the lift for days, never did they mention the bag searchers at the front door nor the four roaming security guards for the rest of the building.

With our finances already under strain this is really

not what we needed to hear, and the pressure really was beginning to take hold of us. We had to see what we could do to strip back some of the hours or numbers in line with predicted busy and quiet times and managed to get the bill down to around £30,000. Still a ridiculous amount of money, especially given that half of these people had to be on site all of the time regardless of the exhibition.

The security guards also got very bold as we got into the run, being rude to customers who were arriving at the last minute, chasing people out of the exhibition earlier and earlier every night so that they could go home early. We had a few complaints like that but nothing like what we would experience with the security.

Then the final nail in the venue coffin and one of the last straws for the business being able to cope with the lack of sponsorship was all the additional invoices. These were for walling – £22,000. £50 a metre for fucking fake walling! We always planned to use some walling to create a walk around exhibition but had to use way more than planned in order to cover up major blemishes on their walls and block out sunlight as their roller blinds were not effective! £9,300 for the use of a billboard, a billboard that they own may I add. And then electrics! Don't even get me started on electrics. £800 to run a PA system outside for a couple of hours for the VIP night. £250 for power to allow Ashley James to do a two-hour DJ set. £700 to power two TV screens in the entrance tunnel and finally £12,000 to power the spotlights!

12 fucking thousand pounds to power the spotlights! Given that all of the lights were highest tech LED low energy lights, I completely fail to see how this was in any way shape or form a justifiable figure. They may as well have put masks on and held us up at gun point as it was absolute robbery.

To put you in the picture £12,000 of electricity is enough power to run the Blackpool illuminations for 15 days! I know our exhibition was good and we didn't hold back on the lighting in order to do the costumes justice but come on.

By the time the exhibition opened its doors on Saturday 28 July 2018, the business was already in financial difficulties. However, based on the blanket media coverage we had received and the projected revenue streams over the next couple of months I decided it was best to continue. It would have been worse if we hadn't opened and let twenty thousand people down, so I am glad we went ahead.

With a huge sponsorship black hole and now ridiculous additional costs, some of which were last minute undisclosed invoices from the venue, the whole situation was about to get really dire. And just to add the cherry on the top there was of course the Big Bus Company and that farce to deal with which resulted in another £15,000 gone from our cash flow immediately.

By the time we had opened the doors we had managed to pay the venue most of the venue hire costs that we had agreed but now they were determined to make life difficult for us, not only that but what they did was completely illegal and had I known better I would have got a lawyer involved sooner.

A lot of money owed out by the company, but we were busy and popular, and every day Manchester was getting more and more popular on the back of it. We would have been able to continue to pay everyone something but..

The venue were overpowering us and every single day they threatened to close the doors of the exhibition if we didn't continue to pay them all the money we had to them for all the additional invoices. This may appear to be normal and some people may think they were entitled to do this. But since they knew our financial situation, what they should have done is provide space to breath and grow in order for the company to bring in more revenue, which would see them get paid in full. This is exactly what all other creditors did. However, what the venue did next, well….

Every morning I or we arrived at the exhibition in order to be open and set up by 10am, it wasn't that hard a job, you had to switch on the music, the lights and power up the ticket scanners whilst making sure staff were there. There was an accountant called Simon that worked for the Business Design Centre who would be there with his 'Face of Doom' asking us what we were going to pay them today. It got to the stage where the venue was literally checking our bank account on a daily basis to make sure that we were not hiding any money. They were getting us to spend at least an hour or more each day showing them income and expenditures, ticket sales (both on the door and online), bank and financial statements and projected numbers for the following days as well as many other things which I can't remember. Also, they got the security guards to spy on us by counting numbers so they could get a rough idea of income each day to ensure we were not hiding any money or paying other creditors.

They took every single penny that we were making and putting it towards their bill. They didn't care that it left us penniless unable to pay the Hilton Hotel or the catering company or any other creditor for that matter. It got so bad that we couldn't keep up with loan repayments and we couldn't pay the PR company even a bit of what we owed them.

Very quickly all of these things start to add up. We paid the venue over £60,000 during our three-week run adding to the £25,000 we had paid them prior to opening. This meant nobody else got anything and every single day the situation got worse and worse for us.

Our phones starting ringing constantly with people chasing us for payments but worse than that, three of the companies we owed money to were on site. The catering company chased me around the building, the Business Design Centre chased me around the building, the onsite printers, the Hilton Hotel and everyone else started chasing us for money.

It was hell! On one hand I had this huge exhibition that I was incredibly proud of. Every time I walked in and saw it, my heart would flutter a little and I would been in my element looking at all the amazing Spice Girls' history. On the other hand, I had people waiting for me every single morning, waiting to take every single penny that I had off me.

It was extremely aggressive tactics especially from a company as big as the Business Design Centre and one which is arguably illegal. We should have been able to pay all the companies a little bit of money and then that way they wouldn't have lost as much money themselves. It would also have freed up some cash flow for PR and Marketing for the Manchester exhibition, which in turn would have made Spice Girls' Exhibition Ltd more money to pay creditors, then have future exhibitions which would have resulted in every creditor being paid in full over a longer period of time. Instead the fat cat got fatter and the smaller companies that couldn't door stop us and empty our banks every day went without as there was no money left over to pay them.

What makes me feel the worst about the financial situation the company ended up in, is not for the big companies like this that could handle the losses but the small companies like Guest List London who worked their arses off for us and we really struggled to pay them anything. I am so sorry to these companies and I wish I could do something to make it right.

If it hadn't been for the failed sponsorship or the venue taking all our money on a daily basis, we would have made sure that everyone got payments of some kind. Had the sponsorship money came through I am confident that the company would still be running today.

We had thousands of people coming to an independent exhibition. It was a great achievement and with the amount of interest we were getting from around the world, the exhibition should be continuing to tour for years to come.

Would have, could have, should have, is not my style but this one sticks in my throat a little. The venue that we had brought an amazing and different style of event to, had become like enemies and we could feel it becoming more and more hostile every day.

Every other company that we owed money to was beginning to freak out a little and of course because we hadn't managed to pay them properly the PR company who had been amazing at their job, getting us interviews in Vogue and all sorts, quite rightly refused to work for us promoting Manchester.

Straight from London we were going to Manchester and of course we wanted to continue the momentum that we had created in London. Unfortunately, that is why we hired Chuff Media, they were the best in the business and had proved that with London. Now how were we going to promote Manchester to the same level with no marketing budget?

The day-to-day running of the exhibition, after we had got past the daily debt collecting, actually went really well and I was thrilled with the reaction the exhibition was getting. Two guided tours a day for 24 days was a lot and I hadn't quite realised the impact that would have on me. Nor did we really factor in the fact that working every single day would eventually take its toll, especially when we had weeks and months without a day off in the lead up to it.

The first time I took a day off and handed the reins over fully was on the last Sunday in London. I was physically broken and had lost my voice completely. I found myself under strict orders to stay at home and rest up for the day. I hated not being at my exhibition even for one day, but it had to be done, I was dead on my feet.

We maybe didn't get a Spice Girl at the launch evening and we are still not 100% if Mel B paid us a visit or not (there is a mention in the guest book from her and I thought I had seen her on the ground floor at one point) what we did definitely get was a few family members through the doors.

Victoria's mum and dad visited one day and of course foolish me didn't realise who they were. I am glad in a way as I think they kind of appreciated that. Her dad walked around the corner as I was on a live stream on Instagram, I asked if he wanted to say hello without realising at first who he was. I did very quickly notice him and quickly turned the camera away from him, he had a little chuckle to himself about it, maybe at the state of my face as I realised it was him.

The other amazing visitor we had was the stunning Natalie Halliwell and her incredibly well-mannered son. They attended on the second Sunday and one of the staff members on the front desk came running up to me to let me know she was in.

I had to go and introduce myself. I was incredibly nervous and was scared that I would of course say something incredibly stupid. As I walked up to Natalie, I could feel my nerves going, I really didn't want to get this wrong, this is Geri's sister and I am pretty sure it might come up in conversation at some point.

I took a breath and half of me stepped up in true Girl Power style whilst the other half of me withered behind the façade. I needn't have worried in the slightest. Natalie is Geri's absolute spitting image and as you talk to her you can hear their voices are as similar as their features. Natalie was really shy and I don't think she really enjoyed the intrusion of me introducing myself.

I asked her to enjoy herself, take as may pictures as

she liked and to come and get me if she wanted to know anything about the exhibition. I also mentioned that I was running a guided tour in an hour and she was more than welcome to join on to it. I never for one second thought she would but…

Natalie Spent over an hour walking around the exhibition looking at all the different stages before coming back to the front desk promptly at 4pm for the guided tour. No pressure on me then, I only had bloody Ginger Spice's sister following me around the exhibition listening to me rabbit on about things that she had lived through. Now I was nervous.

What happened next was not what I expected at all. I knew Natalie was a bit shy about it so when she asked me not to announce to others on the tour I was already on the same wavelength however I was a bit shocked when Natalie showed me a text from Geri, who was on holiday, saying:

"OMG I love it!".

Hold your nerve Alan, play it cool, I tried my best, but it was hopeless, and I am pretty sure how obvious it was that I was fangirling all over this.

Trying to keep it cool on the guided tour I remembered what Nand had told me about panto once, the VIP was only one person that probably hadn't paid for their ticket, it was all the everyday people that had paid their hard earned money that you had to play to and impress. Natalie had insisted on paying, that's not the point, the point is that I owed it to the others on the tour to keep it professional and I owed It to Natalie to give her the same tour as everyone else got.

Natalie would stand at the back of the crowd and take discreet pictures occasionally but was very courteous to the others, the moment my nerve really went was when she started filming me talking about the items on display. I thought she was just filming little videos to maybe show to Geri but no it turns out Natalie was Facetiming Geri live from the guided tour. Here I was in central London showing Geri's gorgeous sister around our exhibition whilst Geri is on the other end of the phone listening to me twitter on about her costumes.

It made me so self-conscious of what I was doing and saying but what an incredible privilege and an incredible buzz. Natalie really couldn't have been lovelier and at the end of the tour we had a chat for ages. We made our way over to the Spice Bus and got some pictures taken inside it beside Geri's poster.

She later sent me the pictures through WhatsApp and posted them on her own Instagram. Natalie still keeps in touch occasionally now and has said we should meet up for coffee sometime. I hope we do as she is genuinely lovely, and I'd be thrilled to go for a coffee and another chit-chat. She's really easy to talk to and I could really see us on a night out putting the world to rights with a few cocktails. Drinks are on me if you ever fancy it Natalie, I'm sure we would have a giggle.

See, for every bit of turmoil that we were having with the venue and with our finances there was the flip side to that, moments like above were pure gold and that I will never be able to repeat again. Memories that I will treasure forever as the moments that the dream I had really was a reality of sorts. Underneath our worlds were falling apart, but on the surface, we were having a great time with some incredible people.

As we approached the end of the run of the exhibition that is when things really started to turn a little bit ugly, with the venue and indeed other companies threatening us with all sorts.

The venue staff, despite door stopping us had always tried to get through the situation but at this point a horrific little man, in my opinion, called Joe Mullee got involved. He appeared to take a dislike to us from the instant we met him and then appeared to become utterly poisonous towards us. I'm pretty sure I threatened him in some way, I don't mean physical threatened to punch him although I would have loved to, but I mean I think he was threatened by me in some way, it's the only way I can explain his reaction. I think that maybe he was unsure of his sexuality, maybe he had lived a closeted lie for years and didn't like that I was so open, maybe he was just an insecure little man in general or maybe my thinking on him is completely wrong. However, there was really no excuses for what happened next under his and Max Bull's authority. Two men that I will do my best to have stripped of any professional memberships they hold.

15

I Want a Man Not a Boy Who Thinks He Can

What happened in the end with the Business Design Centre is beyond horrendous and they should be utterly ashamed of themselves for how they treated me, my staff, my husband but most of all my female PA Alex.

The next part of the story is what happened to us at the end of the London exhibition. We had just under four days to get the exhibition pulled down, moved to Manchester and set up in a new venue before our next launch evening. The Business Design Centre knew this and knew the pull down was going to be slick and quick. They also knew that we couldn't delay anything at all, even by one hour, and they used this to their full advantage, holding us hostage, holding us to ransom and physically attacking us. I could say it in every paragraph I write in this chapter. They should be utterly ashamed of themselves!!

Utterly Ashamed!

We had made an agreement with the director that we

had been dealing with for the full month we had been there, Max Bull. Whilst we hadn't managed to clear off the full balance we owed them, we had made a bloody good go at it paying them £85,000 and with an agreement in place with Max we were all good to go.

The problem was apparently Joe Mullee doesn't agree to what we had proposed and agreed in principal with Max, and nobody thought to tell us that. As far as we knew we had finished the run at the venue and had an agreement in place for the remainder of the balance.

The venue and all the staff of the venue had been made fully aware of how tight our timeline was to move the exhibition. We closed at 8pm and we wanted most of the costumes and memorabilia off the stages and packed in boxes by 10pm.

It was slick, it is one of the slickest things we have ever done as a team. We had about 15 people ready to start packing up at 8pm and as soon as the last person left it started in a proper whirlwind of excitement.

It was a mixture of mission accomplished for London, it had been stressful with different things, the bus, finances, sponsorship etc, but at this point it was satisfaction, mission accomplished, London under our belts now let's get this baby packed up and moved to Manchester.

We had organised for the most amazing company

ever called Simply Business Moves to help us pack up and move the exhibition to Manchester. They were arriving first thing the next morning with a team of 20 guys in order to get the exhibition on the road to Manchester as soon as possible.

The nightmare started with one overzealous, over dramatic security guard called Mark. Mark was a big massive grey-haired guy. He seemed like a gentle giant for the whole month we had been there, and we had loads of fun with both him and all the other security guards over the run. At the end of the day we were bloody paying them.

Mark apparently decided that his loyalty didn't lie with me, the guy paying his wages, but with the venue owners, and as we set to work stripping out all of the costumes and merchandise that we could as quick as we could (which had always been the plan) Mark freaked out about it.

He got on the phone to Joe Mullee, (the weasel looking creature) and told Joe in a panic that we had stripped out the whole exhibition and we were taking it all out of the building. In reality we had boxed up all of the memorabilia and taken around 20 costumes to my car. The whole exhibition takes up a massive 4 or 5, 7.5 tonne trucks, so how the hell he thought we were putting it all in the boot of my hatchback car I have no idea!

You would have thought we were bank robbers taking all of their own personal belongings with what happened next.

It was 9.55pm and it was time for all out of the building. As we got the team together and headed out the exhibition, we got to the entrance tunnel and Mark walked through with at least another five security guards in tow. He was sweating heavily and looked panicked, breathing heavy and refusing to let us leave with the costumes we had in our hands.

Eh? What was going on? We were aware that there was a clause in the contract that allowed them to prevent us from entering the venue by enacting a legal clause which is called a lien. Nobody and I mean nobody has the right to lock you in a building and refuse to let you leave, only the police have that power.

The next thing I knew the security guards were physically pushing at me and refusing to let me leave with the costumes in my hand, and it wasn't long until these huge guys were wrestling the costumes off me, costumes that are worth tens of thousands of pounds, they were literally grappling at them and throwing them to the floor.

There was all sorts of shouting and bawling going on by this point and people were really beginning to get a bit frightened. All of these security guards were huge, and they were now angry at us, man handling us and the costumes, and we had no real understanding why.

Remember as far as we are aware at this point, we

have an agreement to make payments and everything was ok with the management. We hadn't been informed of Joe's intentions to refuse any offers and lock us out of the building, holding us to ransom. At this stage all we knew was these security men who I was meant to be paying for, had all of a sudden turned on us, and were incredibly threatening.

Mark had said to my PA Alex before he came into the exhibition that she better leave before it all kicked off as he didn't want her to get caught up in all the mess.

Alex was of course panicked, took her bag and case and went to leave the building in a rush, I think she thought there was some kind of fire or threat to us. It was all very dramatic and over the top.

Whilst Steven, me and the rest of the team were upstairs surrounded by security guards refusing to let us leave with our belongings, Alex made her way downstairs to the exit.

Lowri, who was supposed to be 'in charge' of the venue, who was around 20 years old and visibly upset by what was going on could do nothing. We asked her to intervene and instead, probably frightened and scared herself she went and locked herself in her office. How dare these men Max Bull and Joe Mullee, leave this young girl to deal with a situation that they were creating. Again, they should be utterly ashamed of themselves, sitting at home drinking wine and relaxing while some 20-year-old, most probably on a shit wage was left to deal with a major situation that you created.

Appalling!

As we argued with the guards upstairs and were being pushed and pulled around, Alex was downstairs having her own horrendous experience.

The guards had decided to lock the doors. So, despite Mark telling Alex to leave the building quickly because it was about to kick off, here she was at the front door locked in. What happened now is the bit I am most disgusted about.

As Alex became increasingly upset at being locked in, the security guards grabbed her bag and suitcase off her, it seems they thought she was smuggling out the whole 5 x 7.5 tonne trucks' worth of exhibition in her suitcase! And so, decided that they were going to search through her personal belongings. There was Alex surrounded by three massive male security guards all shouting at her, all pulling at her bags and keeping her in the building. Quite rightly she was petrified.

We were still upstairs at this time, so I have Alex's account of this and another friend who was there to witness it all.

Steven, me and the rest of the team were upstairs and horrified at what these security guards who we had known for weeks, were doing to us. Steven begged me:

"Just put the costumes down, please let's just leave and we will come back and get it tomorrow."

I am a little stubborn at times and especially in situations like these, here were these guys that I was paying telling me that I couldn't take my own belongings with me. I eventually put them down and we made our way out of the exhibition with a few pushes and shoves from the security guards along the way.

We kept telling Mark that we had come to a deal with Max and that everything was sorted out and that Lowri had agreed for us to take this 20 or so costumes with us. But all he kept saying was:

"You should have paid the fucking money you owed them then."

Two things about this, why the fuck does some hired security guard know anything about anything financial to do with a contract I had with a company he was not directly employed by. There is no way he should have been able to access that kind of information and secondly you would have thought we had stolen money from his own wallet the way he was treating us.

By the time we got to the front desk of the exhibition on our walk out, we could hear screaming from downstairs, it was hysterical screaming like someone was in real trouble, I felt sick as I asked:

"Where's Alexandra?".

The staircases in the venue were relatively open plan so we could hear the commotion before we actually saw it. Alexandra was surrounded by three huge guys, two of whom didn't speak very good English and she was being shouted at as they rifled through her bag, but worse, through her suitcase, tossing aside her underwear and personal products.

Alex was in hysterics by the time we all got down the stairs, and as all of us made our way down the stairs the security guards were quick to allow Alex to pick up her things and pack them back into her bag. Three huge security guards all shouting at and intimidating Alex who is 5ft 3 with heels on, no wonder she was terrified and hysterical and judging by how quickly they backed away from Alex when we got there, the security guards knew fine well what they were doing was wrong.

We asked what was going on and why the doors were locked, telling the guards that they had no right whatsoever to lock us in the building and that all we wanted to do was exit.

The response was:

"Nobody is going fucking anywhere, I don't care what we are allowed or not allowed to do."

Alex was on the phone to Max Bull the director of the

company, crying hysterical and pleading to be let out of the building. Max ignored even Alex's hysterical pleads to be let out and still the guards kept us locked in the building.

With the whole situation completely out of hand we were all now bottle necked at the entrance of the building. Alex, Steven, Me, Josh and at least another four people that were helping us including Samuel (another collector), along with at least seven or eight security guards. It was a boiling pot and a recipe for disaster. We were all petrified and these security guards were trying everything they could to make sure we were terrified. How dare they keep us locked in a building against our will, half of the people there were volunteers that weren't even involved with the business side of things.

The security guard had left his keys lying on the table and nobody was standing beside the locked door. After repeated attempts to get me and my team out of the building and being told we were "going fucking nowhere", I took the opportunity to grab the set of keys from the table.

This really set the security guards off, all I kept saying to them was:

> "Guys all we want to do is leave the building, if you open the door and let us out, I will give you the keys back."

They weren't for budging and just kept getting angrier that I now had a set of their keys.

We had attempted to phone 101 earlier and had got a recorded message about what we should do, send an email to the appropriate person. I'd given up on help from the police at the point, but this was all getting very out of hand and Alex was still petrified as was everyone else.

Phoning the police was a last resort for us, nobody phones 999 without good reason and as Alex was visibly shaken, crying and screaming for help and as we continued to be threatened and held against our will, it fell on my shoulders to resolve the situation. The people who helped me, the people I loved, were frightened and so was I.

In hindsight I wish I had called the police a lot sooner.

"What's going on now sir?"

I could hear the officer on the other end of the phone becoming more concerned as the screaming and shouting seemed to suddenly escalate from that of a moped to that of a huge screeching jumbo jet.

"We need help, they're pushing us around, have locked us in the building and are threatening us."

No sooner were the words out of my mouth when BANG....

I feel a huge force suddenly reach from behind me and from my left-hand side, two security guards have decided to tackle me and as I fight back two more join the mix. Four massive security guards slamming me against the wall, wrestling with me, both arms pinned up my back, pinned against the wall and in agony, the pain in my shoulder which was always dodgy was unbearable and of course they wouldn't let me go.

I remember it being calm whilst it was happening, almost in slow motion with a heightened sense of awareness as to what was around me, what was going on.

It wasn't the pain of being slammed against the wall that stayed with me, nor the screaming of my PA Alex and other helpers, it was the horrific helpless howl of my husband, a look of sheer horror on his face as he screamed my name.

Four security men attacking me whilst two others held back my partner. That look on his face is etched on my mind forever. It's still upsetting to think about it. You protect the people you love and at this moment in time, maybe not directly because of me, but Steven was suffering. He was like a wounded animal, helpless, furious and shaken.

The police must have realised the seriousness of the situation following on from the phone call as it was literally less than two minutes before they had arrived on the scene with blue flashing lights.

In that time though my hands had been cut by the security guards wrestling the keys from me, my shoulder was seized, and we were all visibly shaken by what had just happened.

Never in my life had I been so happy to see blue flashing lights and hear the sound of a police siren getting closer and closer.

As the police pulled up right outside the building Mark unlocked the door and tried to keep us inside whilst he went to speak to them. I made it perfectly clear to him at that time and loud enough so that the police could hear:

> "You have absolutely no right to keep me locked in a building."

I don't know what Mark said to the policeman and to be honest I couldn't care less, when they stepped up to us and asked us to step back inside to discuss it, we all point blank refused. There was no way we were going in that building with those idiots who had just attacked us for absolutely nothing. We were attacked for trying to leave the building.

The first thing the police said to us when we explained what was going on was:

> "This should be a civil dispute, you know we have to deal with people being stabbed right?"

It wasn't aimed at us but the security guards, what the fuck were they thinking letting it escalate to this extent and this stage.

The police took statements from us all, checked my car to see that we hadn't managed to fit the biggest music exhibition ever into the boot of it and insisted that we were allowed to leave.

Poor Alex was in bits around the corner and when I went to see if she was ok, she was hysterically crying, telling me that she hated me. We had all been frightened but Alex was truly petrified by what they had done to her.

We had to sit there at the side of the road in central London and get ourselves calmed down to a state where we could gather our thoughts and move. Steven was dealing with the last of the statements with the police and then he drove the car round to pick us up.

As we started the drive home that night, we were all completely shell shocked at what had just happened.

My first point of call was to Max Bull to ask what the fuck had just happened?

> "We have been told that you stripped out the whole exhibition" said Max.

> "Even if we fucking had Max, we had an agreement between us, what the fuck gives you the right to treat my staff like that, your security have assaulted me and my female PA and you better have an apology and a bunch of flowers for her first thing in the morning."

I hung up the phone to Max as abruptly as I had gone on it, my blood was boiling, and I was shaking with anger and adrenaline. I was crying but not for me but for the whole situation we found ourselves in. The whole financial side had not been ideal, but we had an agreement in place, and this was a horrendous way for us to finish an incredibly successful three weeks in London. Bruised, battered and in shock.

16

Step to Me

It turned out that Joe Mullee had decided that he didn't want to honour the deal that we had struck with Max and instead he was now going to do everything he possibly could to hold us to ransom.

Knowing that our timescales were beyond tight to get to Manchester, Joe decided to enact the Lien, go back on our gentlemen's agreement (fucking weasel), lock us out of the building so that we couldn't do any work and then demand that we paid £10,000 on the spot and also sign personal guarantees, putting our house at risk if we didn't pay them.

They had already asked us what other assets they could take of ours and had we let them I am pretty sure they would have made us sign over our house to them there and then. Instead they used the timescale for our next exhibition to hold us to ransom.

There was no apology the next morning for how we had been treated. Instead they refused to allow the removals company access to the site and so instead we had twenty guys from Simply Business Moves hanging about at the back entrance of the building ready to move the exhibition to Manchester and they were being refused entry.

With bruises and cuts on my hands and with my shoulder visibly painful I really struggled to go to a meeting that morning with the Business Design Centre and their lawyers. Half of me was frightened to go anywhere near the building and the other half of me was frightened what I would do to this guy if I'd seen him without his security guards around him.

Steven went to the meeting with Josh at 9am and we were fully expecting the situation to be resolved by 10am. Steven would go in, they would have a chat and honour the agreement they agreed in principal the day before, they would apologise for the antics the night before and we would be on our way.

No.

Joe Mullee, weasel freak, knew that we needed the stuff out and quickly, so instead of keeping to the agreement, changed the terms and said he wouldn't let us in the building until we paid then £10,000 and both of us signed personal guarantees.

There was absolutely nothing we could do. Every single second that we wasted we got closer and closer to missing the deadline for the opening of the Manchester exhibition in what was now just three days' time. Everything was planned to be so slick and according to the plan me and Alex should be on our way to Manchester by this point along with the first lorry load of stuff.

We waited in an Angel Islington café for Steven to come out of the meeting and tell us that we could get going. We sat there feeling sick, deflated and a little bit scared that one of the security guys would come into the café so we decided to move to a café further away.

Steven eventually phoned and said they were not budging and unless we paid them the money we were not getting in the building.

They knew we had no money, they had been making us empty our bank accounts every single day for the past three weeks, they knew the sponsorship company had let us down, they were still friends with them in business, they had after all rented an office from them for years. They knew that the timescales were tight, and they knew that we were broken.

Hideous hideous men that I wouldn't piss on if they were on fire. When asked about the antics of the night before and if either of them as gentlemen had anything they wanted to say to Alexandra, both smugly replied:

> "No comment" under the instruction of their lawyer.

Happy to talk about taking our house from us but not happy to talk about how you as 'professional gentlemen' had allowed my female PA to be so terrified and attacked under their orders. The same men that had allowed me to be attacked by four security men whilst two others held my partner back.

What do you say now guys? Is it still no comment?

Steven phoned and said they hadn't agreed and we went back and offered them some of the business assets as security. Still they wouldn't budge, they had us over a barrel and they knew it. They didn't care that by stopping us going to Manchester they were actually stopping us from earning money to pay them back anything at all.

They were happy to be creepy little fuckers and that was it they weren't discussing the matter further.

We had no way of securing £10,000. Every avenue that we had, had been exhausted to get the exhibition up and running at all and now we literally had nowhere to go and the clock was ticking. If we missed the opening of Manchester it would cost us around £100,000.

By lunchtime we had to give up and realise that we were not going to get into the building that day. I had to tell the removals company that they couldn't get in and they in turn had to send all of their men home for the day. That delay in itself cost us a total of £4000 in wasted labour, not to mention the hotel rooms that had been booked for Manchester and everything else that went along with it.

We were now going to be at least a day behind and as Steven scurried about trying to get the £10,000 together for me, I was busy trying to arrange the removals for the next day and for the plan to kick in quick smart as soon as we could get any form of access.

After a few frantic phone calls and after discussing options like pawning our wedding rings, especially mine, Steven managed to get a loan secured from a payday lender.

One thing that was our saving grace right there and then was the fact that my Steven is Rain Man when it comes to his finances. He never misses a payment for anything and that coupled with his impressive employment record, he was able to secure what we needed to get the show back on the road.

Steven prides himself on being good with money and he has always helped me to get my finances sorted. What he absolutely hated was having to go to a pawn shop and talk about a loan. It wasn't that he was too proud, he did it and got the loan, but it absolutely broke his heart, and never do you ever want to see your partner cry.

These bastards at the Business Design Centre were making my Steven do the one thing that he despised. 1000% interest on a loan is something that would make Steven sick, but what could we do. There was nowhere to go and even when we told the BDC this they didn't care and were happy for Steven to go and take the payday loan as long as they got £10,000 from us.

What I since found out is that this is around a £17

million pound turnover a year company, so why were they here doing this? There is no other explanation for them acting so unprofessionally, so brutally towards us, other than they made it personal.

Joe had taken exception to us for one reason or another and was doing everything he could to use whatever power he had over us.

My husband may have dipped his head temporarily and wept a little on his way to get that loan, but he is a giant, he would never treat anyone the way we had been treated, not just that, he is very intelligent and whilst he may have been deflated and defeated at this point he was already running rings around these halfwits in his head legally. I was worried though, and as he was on his way to get the loan I had to phone him, tell him I loved him and that I was worried about him. I was genuinely scared he was going to jump in front of a train. We broke our hearts telling each other that it would be okay, that whatever happened we would always be okay.

I have given the venue and these two men Max Bull and Joe Mullee repeated chances to step up and do the right thing. I have asked them both personally to be gentlemen and apologise to Alex for how she was treated. Alex is still waiting.

It's been nine months since the exhibition and neither of these animals has had the ability or decency to do the right thing and my vow now is:

I will make sure the whole world knows how you like to treat woman when you are hiding behind your security guards.

What I also promise is that with every fibre of my being I will ensure that we have our moment in court with you, that we get to tell a judge what you did to us and what you thought was an acceptable way to treat us, whilst hiding behind your eight security guards. I also promise you that I will do my very best to have you struck off from any professional organisation that you may belong to.

All of the above is within a professional remit, do you get it? No security guards threatening you or pushing you guys around, no personal threats of violence (as much as I would like to meet you in a dark alley), a professional vow from me that I will get my personal assistant, the woman that held my hand for months, the woman that gave me idea after idea and helped me bring them to life, the woman that is a military wife with two very young boys to look after, the woman that you slammed against a wall, intimidated and frightened, a woman that is my friend. I will make sure she gets her justice from you. I will make sure that, that horrendous experience that you put her through is not what she remembers from our amazing exhibition.

You are scum bags of the lowest order and I'm coming for you!

Steven, my guardian angel had managed to get the

money together from the loan and we paid it to the venue the next morning.

We had spoken to a lawyer and her advice would have been not to sign the personal guarantees or pay the money but rather apply for an injunction against the Business Design Centre. However, they had us over a barrel and they knew it as an injunction would take at least one week to secure and by that point it would all be too late! Therefore, there was no choice but to pay them the money and sign the guarantees. There was also the police case that we could pursue.

There was no way that we were going to agree to sign anything at the venue itself with the same security guards around that had attacked us two days prior. Instead we met at a local café. We had to ensure that the money had been transferred to their accounts before they would come and meet us. Once that was done they came round to the café.

It was me there to sign the document in person (Steven had signed his previously and was sorting the money out), and Alex and Josh were there for support. Max and Joe walked in late, again, knowing that we were time critical they were doing everything they could to disrupt progress.

When they did walk in, Max asked if we wanted a coffee or anything as if we were going to be friendly with him whilst he was blackmailing us to sign over our entire lives.

We signed the forms and asked them to ensure that

none of the security guards were anywhere near us. We asked if they would let the removals company into the loading bay now and they agreed.

Max went to shake hands, I laughed at him and walked away but it was Joe's reaction that had us all laughing by the time we left the café. Pathetic excuse for a man had looked to Alex as an ally and what a mistake that was. By the time it came to him signing the paper he was shaking and looking at the ground, utterly ashamed of himself and so he should be.

Alex had insisted on being there that morning, I love Alex to bits for this, she was never going to let these two men get the better of her and in true Girl Power style Alex held her head up high and looked them right in their eyes. Neither one could look her in the face and whilst she was shaking like a leaf when she walked out that café, she was incredibly proud of herself for facing up to them, and so she should be.

My Steven and my Alex have more dignity in their little fingers than these two scumbags have in their entire bodies. What was a business contract and arrangement, had been made entirely personal by them and resulted in physical injury to us.

For the last time in this book. Shame on you and to the Business Design Centre who still employ these two men, shame on you.

By the time we walked around the corner, into the Business Design Centre and up to the exhibition rooms, the removals guys were already in the room and moving things around. They had been on standby all day the day before and for a couple of hours already that morning. They were beyond keen to get the job done.

From the ashes of the last few days, from having the utter shit kicked out of us to now having our whole team plus a team of twenty removals guys all pumped up and raring to go, it couldn't have been a more Jekyll and Hyde situation.

We were down and out, physically, emotionally and financially broken, but we had a job to do and we were behind by over 24 hours.

The Manchester venue was starting to get really twitchy that we were not going to show up and who could blame them. After a quick phone call to put their mind at ease, it was back to the job in hand and we had to pack like we had never packed before.

17

Lift Me Up

It wasn't easy picking ourselves up off the floor, we had literally been bruised and battered, financially we were under a lot of pressure and now we had less than two days to get an exhibition packed up, moved up to Manchester and ready to launch.

We were also so drained physically and emotionally that I didn't actually think it was ever going to be possible.

Something happens when the team is all together. I suppose it's a bit like that Spice Girls' buzz, we all feed off each other and when one of us is struggling the others rally round to get us up and on with the job.

Packing up was going to be a struggle and so was time but right there at that moment, somehow, we put everything out of our minds, put our heads down and worked slicker and faster as a team than we had ever done before. It wasn't the first time and was by no means going to be the last time.

The thing about good friends and good staff is that when the chips are down, they are there for you and there to pick you up out of the mud. If it wasn't for Alex Maughan that day, I think we would have given up on getting to Manchester.

Alex gave me a talking to, told me that everyone was looking to me to get on with the job, to gee us up and say:

"Come on we can do this"

Within a couple of hours most of the exhibition costumes and memorabilia were all packed up in boxes and ready to go into the van and on their way to Manchester.

I don't know how we did it but at this stage the plan was for me to leave everyone else to get the rest of the stuff packed up whilst I made my way to Manchester to meet the first lorry load there.

From rock bottom to absolute elation, the first van was packed up and ready to go and we were on our way at exactly the same time as it.

We stopped to film the 20 guys from Simply Business Moves doing what they did best. Without these guys Manchester would never have happened, neither of the Manchester exhibitions actually. It was total euphoria. They had been held back for just over 24 hours and were ready to prove to us just how bloody good they were. It was slick, they were a lot of fun and unlike some workman they had more than one gear. When the going was tough these guys got their heads down, sweated their guts out and got the job done quicker than anyone ever could have.

Once again Josh stepped up and was left behind at the venue to get the last of the staging, mannequins and everything else packed into the remaining trucks. He managed this in record time and then got the train up to Manchester to help up us begin the set up there.

Josh is a funny one. He's been my friend since we lived in Cyprus. One day he turned up to live with his parents who were our next-door neighbours. He's very talented both as a singer and as a guitarist but lacks the belief in himself. A really old smoothie soul with blues tones to his voice it wasn't long until we were gigging together in Cyprus and having great fun doing what we both loved. Singing our hearts out. We really became good friends and like all good friends we can go through months of not speaking to each other and pick up exactly where you left off.

Josh had moved to Uni in Liverpool and then by chance we moved there with Steven's job. When it came time to move to London Josh had finished Uni and he moved down to London with us to help us out and maybe get a few gigs going again. The gigs never happened but Josh really became a part of the family, he'd go up to his bed at night and say "Goodnight dads" to Steven and me. We already loved this boy to bits but there is a real fondness there now. He really is like a little boy we both like to look out for, and he knows it, not only that but this boy has our back and we know it.

There is absolutely nobody else in the world other than Steven that I would have left behind and trusted to get the job done. Josh knows I'm a pain with things and particularly with how I want things done. He knew the plan inside out and helped us put it together.

Fresh out of Uni, the hairy man-child proved exactly what he is capable of. Nothing for us to worry about at all, Josh smashed it out the park with the guys from Simply Business Moves and I don't think he has ever known how much that meant to us. Legend!

Alex and I headed from the venue back to our house in Pinner briefly to pick up Steven and the rest of the costume pieces that had to go up to Manchester. It was a short detour and it wasn't long until we were thankfully on the road out of London.

Steven had been at home most of that morning frantically trying to sort out some kind of money situation. We were flat broke. The venue had taken every single penny that we had and had even insisted upon us taking a payday loan in order to pay them a further £10,000.

At this point the PR company Chuff media were of course also chasing us for payments towards the outstanding balance that we owed them and of course there was no money in the bank. We'd just been held to ransom.

gassProductions were exactly the same. We owed them some money from the filming of London and now we were struggling to pay them.

This is really where the company itself starts to struggle a little. Up until this point we had always been able to believe that the company as a business was going to be hugely successful, even despite the massive shortcomings of Slingshot we were sure we could plug the whole and get it all back on track.

Had we been able to pay gassProductions and Chuff Media even a few thousand pounds we would have been able to run just as successful a media campaign for Manchester as we had run for London. However, with no money in the bank how could we possibly justify taking on more debt with these companies, and actually quite rightly there was no way these companies were going to do further work to then invoice at a later date.

Chuff Media were the first to pull the plug and said there is no way they could run another campaign for us without at least some payment and so we had a Manchester exhibition that was attracting some coverage off the back of the London exhibition but that would now not have its own campaign.

To be fair on the guys at Chuff they absolutely smashed it out of the park for us with the London campaign. We were on every single radio station up and down the country, then there was interviews with Vogue, Rolling Stones and God knows who else.

The 4.30am dashes to the TV studios were also all

down to Chuff, the interviews with Dan Wootton and Christine Lampard on the Lorraine Kelly show, the interviews on teatime television, all down to Chuff and of course helped along by all the Spice Girls' hype.

gassProductions were unfortunately in the same position. If there were no payments, then they simply couldn't come and film the launch and the exhibition. They couldn't take any more risk on us than they already had.

gassProductions; Andy Smith and his team are all bloody amazing and I would love to be able to count them as friends for life.

Andy and I went to the Isle of Wight to film with the Spice Bus at the harbour marina. It was the first time I had ever seen the bus and he managed to capture the total excitement of the moment. Andy is a gentleman; someone you would want to call your friend although he can be a grumpy bugger at times. Ha!

Whilst we were totally gutted the he wouldn't be there to film it all and to get more footage for the documentary, I totally understood his position. He knew the sponsorship company had messed things up for us. He had given us feedback on how hopeless they had been. Andy was desperate to be involved as a sponsor but said:

> "Kieran couldn't seal the deal and that he was very disinterested in talking about anything."

That it was either

"""5k or no sponsorship involvement."

This just doesn't work on every level and there were other ways that Andy could have been a sponsor. I was shocked to hear how bad Andy's experience with Kieran had been.

Still, not having Andy there was hard, even as a mate I could have done with him being there. He'd been so heavily involved in the process that I had actually began to rely on him to keep me right and tell me what to do and where to do it.

I had the easy job, most of the time with press all I had to do was talk about the Spice Girls and my collection of memorabilia and costumes. I could do that all day every day so that bit of it was very natural.

To stop fidgeting, to sit still, not to pick my nose on film (haha only kidding) but you get the gist, that was all Andy. He told me how to speak, how to stand, how to look past a camera etc. He taught me so much and I will always be forever grateful for that. He was an extension of the Spice Girls, a Spice Boy, teaching me to believe in myself and that I should be confident with the camera as I can do it reasonably well. This was priceless and still stands me well with interviews. Thanks Andy ya big hunk haha! What happens in IoW stays in IoW #Gayforaday! I'm totally only joking of course but I hope if any of your friends read this that you get slagged for life. You are a gentleman buddy!

So, despite the lack of PR and the loss of our crew to put it out over socials professionally, we had to get ourselves up for this and believe in it.

I think Steven, Alex and I were all as equally as relieved as each other to be leaving London that day. Whilst we still had a massive battle ahead of us to save the business and exhibition at least it couldn't be worse than what we had just experienced.

We were still numb, still genuinely shocked and it seemed like one thing after another. Leaving London behind us in the mirror, literally, I could feel us all starting to relax a little more with each mile away we got.

The security guards that attacked us would not be in Manchester, nor would the pitiful directors that ran the set up. It was a fresh start for us.

Of course there was no sponsorship in place at all for Manchester despite the fact that it was meant to have been secured by Slingshot Sponsorship, no surprise that there was nothing in place, but with costs a lot different we were still, even at this point, confident we could make it work.

There were moments in that journey where we chatted about what we were going to do with Manchester. There were moments where we all cried about what we had been through, taking time to take stock and tell each other it's ok and that we love each other.

I'm sure we probably argued over a couple of things as well but when it is this kind of tense situation you do, and these are not the things you remember, the petty arguments or squabbles. What you remember is the solidarity. The hurt but more importantly the will to heal and to make each other better, to make the situation better and still having the belief in each other to push forward.

The car was cramped, and poor Alex was stuck in the back with a car full of Spice Girls' costumes piled up around her. Unable to move, cramped, tired, hungry, missing her family and upset, somehow Alex managed to keep herself together and plough on. Warrior Woman.

18

Bumper to Bumper

How do you even begin to pull off the biggest task of your life, again, when you are running on empty from doing it the first time. Not only that but with the shit kicked out of us.

It's simple really, you have an amazing team around you who believe in you even if they don't believe in the project that they are working on. The team are so special to me and are my best friends in the world so when I dipped my head, they kicked me up the arse and vice versa.

Nothing and I mean nothing that we have achieved has ever compared to the Manchester build, nothing compares to what we managed to pull off at Manchester Central.

Running a full 36 hours behind schedule and with less than 24 hours to go until we hosted our launch party, it really was going to take something special to make #SpiceUpManchester any kind of possibility.

On top of all of that, with the financial situation so awful, we had only just managed to pay the venue enough money for them to allow us to go ahead and they were putting a lot of trust in us. There was no budget for marketing, no budget for PR, no budget for fancy standalone walls or individual spotlights like in London and until we actually got there, we had no real idea how it was going to look in the space.

The Manchester venue are and were amazing, and Manchester gave us all a real treat with a whole completely new vibe that we hadn't anticipated. The city is completely different and much more relaxed than London. The people don't take anything in life too seriously and instantly whether it was the relief of being away from London, we were having a lot more fun already.

Steven, Me and Alex got there around 8.30pm on the Wednesday evening (VIP Launch evening was starting at 7pm the next day!) and we were so happy to meet the staff guy that was on duty that night. I think it helped that he was extremely handsome and I'm sure it was Alex or one of the Alexes who took great delight in pointing out how peachy his bum was.

For the life of me I can't remember his name (I've left this in as it is funny, his name was Alex, another bloody Alex) but we had so much fun with him that night, we were all so exhausted and hyper in equal measures and here was this handsome man cracking jokes with us offering to fix whatever he could for us. It couldn't have been more chalk and cheese from what we had just come from.

He was meant to be going home at 10pm and had been on shift since about 7am that morning. It was the only thing he was cranky about, but we kept being hyper and overtly fun and cracking Spice Girls' jokes with him. The vans were running so late (Business Design Centre's fault) and we were having to do our best to sweet talk this guy into staying later and later.

He eventually agreed to stay on until midnight but that was the final line, and everything had to be in the building and the building doors locked by this point.

The first thing we had to do when we got to Manchester was put a brave face on and smile for the camera. We had arranged a media interview with the wonderful Belinda Scandal (an amazing drag mama from Manchester, you should check her out if you are in the city) for a Manchester Gay social media channel associated with Canal Street.

By this point of course half of the exhibition was meant to be built and they were meant to be filming the making of the exhibition in Manchester. Without any lorries of staging or memorabilia the only thing we had with us was the actual costume pieces and some coat hangers.

We had to make the most of what we had and to be fair on Belinda that is exactly what she did. She used the open space as a catwalk and instead of talking about the vast exhibition we focussed in on a few of the key costume pieces. This is the thing with media, there is always best laid plans but sometimes in fact most of the time things don't go quite to plan and you have to wing it to an extent.

I can't say thank you enough to the guys from Canal Street: Ian, Belinda, Michelle and all the others for all of the amazing help you gave us and of course it was always the most fun ever. There was never a hassle with these guys, constantly cracking jokes, slagging each other off.

Belinda also had size eight platform boots on, sky high proper Geri style boots with a Union Jack dress and full-blown Ginger Spice hair. I have never been able to try on a pair of buffalos because I have size 9 feet but here, I was with the chance to put actual Ginger Spice's platforms on (well at least the extremely glamorous drag queen version of her).

This is one of the weirdest experiences ever and not one that I would really rush to do again. It felt weird being that much taller than I was and I was a little bit unsteady on my feet. Of course, it wasn't easy to walk in massive shoes and must take some real practice, but it wasn't for me. I loved the experience but now I've done it I can't say I will not be rushing out to buy myself a sky-high pair of buffalos. Fun for five minutes.

After Belinda and the team had finished filming the material that they needed and whilst we waited, biting our nails as to whether the vans were going to get there on time, we discovered that the curtains on rails (that were already installed and in place in the venue) acted as a perfect pathway for an exhibition and so solved the problem of not having any actual partition walling. On top of that the venue had managed to find us six big uplighters, which added mood lighting to the curtains perfectly. We used five, one for each Spice Girl of course.

We also discovered that the lighting in the main hall was able to dip and act as spotlights in certain areas as well. Oh my God, this venue was incredible, and they were already going way above and beyond what we had expected of them.

Here we were at our new venue in Manchester, shitting ourselves in case the lorries didn't turn up but everything we were touching was turning to gold for us. Finally, some good luck coming our way and instantly it was changing our mood, giving us more energy and we were bouncing ideas off each other.

All that we could do until the lorries arrived was literally anything that we could, measure up, tidy up, check out power points, exit points and any of the other boring jobs. We set up the front desk with books and got to know the building.

At 10.30pm the first of the lorries arrived and it was straight to work with the couple of guys that had arrived with it.

It didn't take us long to empty the first couple of lorries as they were full of built up staging and in the grand scheme of things the staging is one of the easier things to move, especially if it is built up. The other lorry had some merchandise and costumes, and this always takes longer. It's all in smaller boxes, is actually heavier and you have to take a lot more care and attention with them.

Even still, that van was emptied in no time and it was back to biting our nails and hoping that the other vans were going to make it on time.

There were eight vans in total and some of them were at risk of not being able to unload until the next morning due to potentially arriving after midnight or due to not quite making it as far as Manchester before having to park up due to driving regulations.

We couldn't stand about doing nothing so we set about getting staging and anything that we could into place. Even though it was late, and every part of our bodies ached, we couldn't stand about and waste a single minute.

Every phone call from the lorries on route made us more and more nervous that they weren't going to make it and even if they did, we would not have enough time to get them unpacked before midnight.

On the plus point we already had a skeleton of the exhibition in place. Some staging was all set out, some mannequins dressed, some display stands out in their correct place and some boxes of merchandise placed where they needed to be unpacked. It was much slicker than London already. Of course, the boxes had all been packed in stages, so there was no sorting it out like London.

Five past eleven, ten past, twenty-five past and this guy was really getting twitchy:

> "We are going to have to wait until the morning to unpack the lorries guys."

Oh no, this was our first nightmare in Manchester, the lorries that were on their way had to turn around and leave for another job as soon as they were unloaded, they were needed for another job and were switching drivers as soon as they got there.

Half past eleven, twenty-five to 12 and three of the final four lorries finally arrived.

We now had twenty-five minutes to get more than half of the exhibition unloaded from the lorries and into the venue. We had a huge team to do this, as with the lorries also arrived a team of guys from Simply Business Moves to supplement the team that arrived earlier that evening. It seemed like an impossible task but with everyone still buzzing despite exhaustion, I got the team together with the removal guys and said:

> "This is where we can catch up, this is what can make or break this exhibition in Manchester. I know we are all tired, but we have twenty minutes to do the impossible. Grab whatever you can and get it in the building, it doesn't need to be placed

> anywhere specifically, just get it in the door in one piece."

Or something to that effect.

What happened next is single-handedly my favourite thing that has ever happened with the exhibition!

Never have I been so proud of the team around me and never have I been so amazed by such a mammoth team effort.

Every single one of us there that night pulled together to make this 20 something strong crowd of people, a force to be reckoned with. There is footage of it somewhere, I'll need to try and look it out, it's phenomenal what we achieved.

Three massive huge vans full of Spice Girls' merchandise, staging, hundreds literally hundreds of mannequins and everything else that you could possibly imagine associated with the exhibition.

Even the guy from Manchester Central pitched in and helped, he even said he couldn't believe what he was seeing in front of him. All these people that hadn't stopped working since 7am that morning were giving us every single thing they had in the tank.

And it worked.

With two minutes to spare we all stood back and gave ourselves the biggest cheer ever, high fiving each other and hugging it out.

The nightmare of London and the piggery of the venue seemed like a million miles away. Here was the team absolutely smashing it, proving that we were made of strong stuff, that it would take more than a bump in the road and a small weasel like man to keep our team down for long.

We were all so passionate about the project and it was infectious, whatever we were doing we tried to do it with fun, a spring in our step and our tongues firmly in our cheeks, much like the Spice Girls back in the 90s. We made people like us, made people listen to the plan and what we were doing and in turn that whole vibe rubbed off. It was completely infectious.

Here we are at midnight, making it by the skin of our teeth, all of the stuff was in the venue (except from one last small van load), we had celebrated our accomplishments and even the grumpy guy from Manchester Central was laughing and smiling with us. Only joking Alex, you know you did us proud that night and we could never thank you enough.

It was a much-needed boost for us all. I know I keep saying it but up until this point we were not sure if Manchester was going to go ahead. We were absolutely broken as a team, both physically and emotionally, but we refused to give in.

> "If you work hard and try hard you can achieve anything."

That's what the Spice Girls taught me and that is

what I live my life by. Another quote that I like, and I am sure it was from Geri in the 90s:

> "It's not how you get knocked down that counts, it's how you get back up that matters."

I'd rented a two-bedroom flat just a 10-minute walk away from the venue, it was gorgeous, not extravagant by any means, but it was a little bolt hole for us all to retreat to. I don't think at the time I had realised just how packed it was going to be in the flat. I maybe hadn't thought it through properly.

I can't believe I have not mentioned the gorgeous Georgia before now. Georgia was an essential part of the team and became my absolute rock on a day-to-day basis. I couldn't love Georgia more and I don't think she quite realises just how much she means to me.

Georgia is a crazy, bonkers, unique individual in the true sense of it. Wacky, hyper intelligent, knowledgeable, deep, silly, and absolutely my kind of person. Georgia dances to her own tune and doesn't give two fucks what anyone thinks about her. She has strong beliefs and an equally strong sense of feminism, Girl Power and achievement. There are not enough words to describe how fabulous Georgia is, but thank God she had arranged her own accommodation for those first few days at least. A God send in every way, much like both Alexes.

In the flat that night was Steven and me in one

bedroom, Alex Lodge and Josh sharing the other bedroom and Alex M on the sofa. The little flat was overflowing.

I can't remember what we did that night, I'm pretty sure it was home and straight to bed in order to try and get ourselves together early the next morning but to be honest I have no definitive memory of it. I'm sure we all struggled to get to sleep as it was a new flat, we had too much on our brains and were still reeling from the events of London beneath the surface, but at the same time we had a job to do. However, the exhaustion finally set in and finally I swear I slept like a baby for a few hours, we all must have, or we would not have got through the Thursday with the style and finesse that we did.

I do remember waking up the next morning having only had those few hours' sleep and feeling every single part of my body aching and being overtired. Do you know that kind of tired when you are awake but definitely not with it or functioning properly? You know that kind of tiredness where you feel physically sick and you walk into a wall or a bathroom door, that.

Steven is good on days like this as he is Mr super organised, he gets us up and organised with everything we need for the day whilst I get myself ready, have a morning smoke (disgusting), a can of red bull (which I have now stopped) and a shower to try and wake myself up.

I'm filling in the blanks from what I presume I did. All I really remember from that morning was being sore all over and knew we had another massive day ahead of us. Literally we had about 8 or 9 hours to build the exhibition before the VIP Launch evening.

Anyway, up and at it first thing in the morning, it wasn't long until we were neck deep in Spice Girls' merchandise and memorabilia. Some of the feedback about this is that it was a bit like a jumble sale. The thing is it's also what most visitors absolutely loved. It's hard to make 3000 odd items of merchandise look structured but still fit it all in. It wasn't about the way it was displayed but as a whole display it was meant to show just how enormous the scale of the merchandise was.

The memorabilia and merchandise are the parts that everyone owned, you maybe didn't have all the dolls from a collection, but every single person could point to at least one item in the exhibition and say 'I had that' or 'I remember my sister had that'. It was the sheer volume of merchandise that people couldn't believe. Thousands of items from my collection and thousands of items from Liz's collection and it literally took hours to lay out in any way, never mind some kind of displayed structured exhibition-style lay out.

The final lorry also arrived first thing and we had it all to set up all over again but this time it was different. Even though we were about 36 hours behind schedule with only 8 or 9 hours left to the VIP opening night it felt different. It was the second time we were doing it, we knew where everything had to go, not just in my head this time but the whole team knew roughly where things were to be placed. Also, we didn't need to wait for deliveries and spend time building staging, display stands or rope barriers as they were all moved from London fully built.

Somehow, and I have no idea how, but the Manchester exhibition at Manchester Central starting taking shape out of nowhere. There were people making sure the mannequins were out, people making sure the stages were out, people lifting and moving all the boxes to where we needed them to be and by lunchtime that day all the vans were unloaded, all the stages were in place, all the mannequins were built and it was time to start putting the costumes out and memorabilia out.

With the costumes in place we had an exhibition of sorts and even if we didn't manage to get every item of memorabilia out on display then at least the most important aspect was there. It really was down to the wire and every minute that passed felt more and more precious.

By about 2pm of that second day in Manchester it was all really taking shape, most of the costumes were out, the Spice Girls' themed bedroom was sorted, the boys had sorted out all the rope barriers and information posts. We were not out of the woods yet and there was still so much work to get done in the next few hours to get the exhibition ready for the launch evening. We hadn't even really touched the merchandise in the boxes.

Regardless of the state of the exhibition we had realised previously that there is a time when the team have given you everything that they possibly can and by mid-afternoon of that second day, that was the moment. I was ready to call it a day and let everyone get ready for VIP Launch evening – we would have to launch in its current state then come in early the next morning to finish off before opening to the public.

However, given the layout of Manchester, somebody suggested that if we could finish all the Spice Girls' stages for the VIP night, we could block off the Solo, Viva Forever and Designer stages with curtains to finish them in the morning. So that is exactly what we did. By about 4.30pm all the Spice Girls' stages were finished, and I was ready to send everyone away to get ready. But the team had other ideas...

A final Herculean effort by the team in the final 90 minutes saw all stages complete (with some minor exceptions to be completed the next day) and all empty boxes, rubbish etc. dumped in a storeroom.

Manchester was already completely different, even the staff were pitching in and were a million times more helpful. Grabbing empty boxes and moving them to the storage rooms or sweeping the carpets and tidying up in general, it was all helping.

Liz came to help us build in Manchester. She was

aware that we were well behind schedule and had offered to help. I knew it was hard for her with a young kid, but I was happy to have more hands on-deck.

There was one problem with that though. We were established as a team by this point and I know that Liz has a completely different style of working from me. Liz will admit that she is super in control of absolutely everything and has a micro-management style. I didn't and don't have that kind of style, I trust the people around me to do what they are doing and will help if it is needed.

We also have completely different ways of speaking to people. I like to keep things on a friendly scale throughout anything that I do whereas Liz is much more direct and can at times come across as being incredibly rude. I have always taken it with a pinch of salt and learned over time to bark back at Liz in the same way as she can dish it out. I'm like that with everyone and very much try to mirror how people are.

I had to have a conversation with Liz that day before she came down. It was a bit awkward and to be honest I am not sure if it was needed or not but my staff team had worked so bloody hard and the last thing they or I needed was for Liz to come in, micro-manage and correct anything that was maybe slightly out of place.

I think Liz was little offended by the conversation,

but I couldn't risk upsetting my staff team in any way. They had worked so hard, were on a roll and I couldn't interrupt it.

Whether it was the conversation we had or whether it was always the plan, it couldn't have been more different. Liz came down to the venue asked what we needed done and simply got on with it as a member of the team. It helped immensely and with the extra help and Liz's knowledge of the collection it took the pressure off me a little.

Like we always did, we also had a little unexpected miracle guardian angel. This time it was in the form of Hugo MaCqueenie. I can't remember how I met or was introduced to Hugo. I think maybe he messaged me and asked to be involved, like so many others.

He wanted to present the VIP evening but more than that he just wanted to help in any way that he could. He was getting great promo out of it but at the same time he really went above and beyond.

That day he turned up in his usual whirlwind style, introduced himself to the hunky boys helping us out in typical Hugo fashion and then got stuck into helping us.

Hugo, his friends, Alex M and Georgia all got stuck into the VIP bags and got them sorted out for the launch evening. Hugo had also managed to secure vouchers for all sorts to put into the bags and turned up with lots of treats, including pride themed flowers for me for the launch. I love flowers and love sending people flowers, we should all do it more often, not only do you get the nice surprise when you receive the flowers but every time you look at them you see the kind act and think of the person who got you them.

Josh and his two friends from Manchester who were helping us out, were now outside sorting out the pink carpet for the entrance, along with the barriers and rope posts.

Alex M and I left the team to get everything put away, all that was really left were empty boxes and the last few bits and pieces. There was no way I was making the same mistake as the London launch, turning up looking like a bank manager. We left a little earlier so that I could do a quick shop and Alex would have time to get ready comfortably. Turns out Alex doesn't need any time to get ready and looks flawless pretty effortlessly. She was ready in ten minutes.

I, on the other hand, take a little bit longer than I like to think I do to get ready. We managed to pick up a pair of checked cropped, pretty tight fighting trousers and a slim fit shirt (which I haven't been able to wear for years). It seems a real bonus of being so run off your feet is that you miss more than the odd meal and the weight falls off.

As soon as I had bought the navy slim fitted shirt and my gorgeous cropped 30" waist trousers, we jumped in a taxi straight back to the apartment, it was pissing with rain and we were starting to worry about time, we were knackered and so it was a little bit of indulgence to save some time. Taxi!

19

Northern Star

We were all in the flat getting ready together, so it was a little bit crazy and manic. We had some alcopops and a drink or two to get us all in the mood. After the achievement of getting it all built, we were absolutely buzzing.

After the trauma we had faced of the last week I insisted to the team that they had the best night that they could, let their hair down and enjoy themselves. They had worked their asses off for me, given me more than anyone should ever have to and now it was time to be proud.

It was a completely different vibe again from the London launch a month earlier. It was much more relaxed, and everyone was so friendly.

We got a taxi to the venue (no bus going the wrong way this time) and when we got there, there were paparazzi waiting for people to arrive. It was so nice to stand and pose a little on the pink carpet with my team with me, Alex, Alex and of course my little superhero Steven.

This is one of my favourite moments of the whole experience. It's a shame Josh and Georgia weren't in the photo but the photo of the four of us on the pink carpet in Manchester, the selfie that one of us took, probably me, is my favourite of the whole experience. We genuinely look happy to be there together as a team. I think that you can see in the picture, despite what has gone on, we are all delighted to be there on that pink carpet, together.

London had been amazing but in a very London official way, this was much more laid back and fun with a less formal vibe and from the minute we stepped foot into the building it was crazy fun.

Hugo MaCqueenie standing in front of the branded photo wall was doing an amazing job of going live to our Twitter feed, covering the event. Hugo was so camp, Manchester is so camp, and it was so much fun. We stood there having a chat with Hugo and I could tell how nervous he was but also, he was like an excitable puppy, camp, in your face and brilliant. Thanks Hugo you did an amazing job of hosting that evening!

Once inside, the venue had done an amazing job at creating Spice Girls' cocktails and providing a cool bar, some people maybe enjoyed the bar a little bit too much, Alex Lodge, but more about that later....

By the time we got there, there were already guests, so it was straight into mingling, smiling for pictures and doing all the other meet and greet things that I absolutely love. I love meeting new people, hearing their stories and finding out about their lives. People are interesting and not one of us is the same. I find that intriguing.

It wasn't long until familiar faces were turning up to talk to me about the exhibition. Sometimes it would take you a second to realise who it was, or it would only be on hearing the introduction name that you would realise who the person was. It was more chilled and friendly but there was half the cast of Coronation Street, some really well-known Manchester faces, influencers and everyone that we would have wanted from the local social scene.

With no PR company working with us we had been a little bit stressed about whether we would get coverage that we really needed but here we were with the who's who of Manchester with the Manchester press snapping everyone as they arrived and chatting away to everyone inside.

For the first time in over a month, Steven and I and indeed the whole team, let their hair down a little that evening. Not so much that we took it too far but enough that it really helped to release some of the stresses of the past month. Manchester was cool and away from London we were all more relaxed and felt more secure. It already felt like so much more fun.

Before I knew it, it was time to give the introductory speech and declare the exhibition open, we invited the celebrities and invited guests to go and take a first glimpse of the new look exhibition. We waited with bated breath to the reaction but there was no need.

It was instantly a hit and the new more open plan layout was also popular. Everyone was enjoying the cocktails and taking loads of pictures with the costumes and of the exhibition in general. Everyone was laughing, copying the dance routines, posing with posters and generally having a great time.

For any launch event this is exactly what you want. It would be horrific if people turned up and didn't actually have fun or want to take any pictures with anything. Instead everyone was striking the Girl Power pose or pouting and pointing just like the Spice Girls. When people are having fun, I am having fun, and this really is a fond memory of the whole experience.

There were a couple of people who were enjoying the cocktails a little bit too much and I am sure one or two people had to be asked to leave because they were a little bit wobbly on their feet. No hassles though and certainly no hilarious cat fights like the ridiculous handbags in London.

Alex Lodge was on great form and knocking the cocktails back like nobody's business. The boy has worked his arse off for me from the minute he has been involved and he is just as passionate about it as I am, maybe even more so. If anything was to happen to me and I didn't have to sell off the collection I would leave it all to Alex. I love you darling boy, you are incredible but that doesn't mean I am not going to tell the story haha!

Hugo gave a lovely closing speech at the end of the night and then presented me with the gorgeous flowers he had brought earlier and no sooner had I opened the exhibition than it was time to thank everyone for coming along and inviting them on to a nightclub for the after party.

In all the frantic activity of setting up Manchester, I can't remember what the club was called, but they had agreed to host the after-show party for us for free, the bar wasn't free but still it was a bit of fun:

> "We aren't paying (we couldn't), but you are more than welcome to come and join us for a drink at the nightclub just around the corner."

A few people did join us at the club, George Samson, The Malones from Gogglebox and a few of the local reporters. Steven and I were shattered and hadn't really got into the whole drinking vibe of the night. We sat happily chatting to people, including Dane 3001 (designer of Mel B's catsuit). Dane is a very proud transvestite and I have to say looks incredible dressed as a woman. I'd do it all the time if I looked like that Dane!

It was clear at the club that Steven and I were not going to hack the pace, so whilst it was less than convenient when Alex Lodge was out of the game, we were glad of the excuse to duck out earlyish.

After drinking half of his body weight in cocktails Alex was very quickly a little bit worse for wear after the fresh air walk to the club. He lay back on his chair unusually quiet and began to fall asleep in the club. The part of the club we were at was outside next to the canal and I begged Alex to get up and move but no...

Alex woke up from his few moments of sleep and projectile vomited everywhere, the one thing he did have the sense to do was point his head towards the ground, thank God, if he hadn't it would have been a scene from The Exorcist.

> "Right Alex, stand up and walk over to the canal and be sick over there, come on son."

If looks could have killed I would have been dead there and then. Alex looked up with nothing but hatred and sheer contempt as if to say:

> "I am fucking ill and I am going to kill you if you say one more word," hehehe this really made me properly chuckle.

What wasn't funny was the sheer amount of vomit that Alex is able to omit from his body. Alex is a big strapping lad but bloody hell I have never seen anyone be that sick.

Of course, the security were over at us within two minutes asking Alex to leave. It was our perfect excuse to duck out early, so Steven and I volunteered to get him home. It was my job anyway, he's just a young boy and no wonder he was sick, not just with the amount of alcohol, but his body was more than exhausted from his recent efforts in getting Manchester set up.

Every two steps we took back from the club, Alex would have to stop to be sick again and I was beginning to think I was going to be up all night looking after him.

We were still all on good form, with Alex even chipping in the occasional joke on the way home, so please don't worry Lodgy, it had no impact on our evening and we are only jealous that we are not that young and carefree.

With Alex tucked up in bed and a bucket beside him, Steven and I took a minute to realise just how amazing the night had been, not just that but how amazing it was that we had managed to get to Manchester at all, and even more incredible than that just how hard our amazing, gorgeous team had worked to make it so.

I can never thank you guys enough! That was Team Spice Up's finest hour. Clubbing together in the worst of circumstances to "work hard and try hard to achieve anything". Just like the Spice Girls taught us.

20

Maybe

The first day of the Spice Up Manchester exhibition was a stark contrast to the franticness of the previous few days leaving London and setting up, a contrast to the heads down and get the job done mentality. It was a relief to have the exhibition set up and running but immediately it was a crash back to the reality of the situation we were in.

There was no money in the bank and we needed this to be a huge success for us in order to make up for the troubles in London.

That first initial day was busy for us and right from the start there was a steady stream of people arriving to see the exhibition. It wasn't on the same scale as London, but we hadn't had the same PR and marketing campaign and at this stage it was looking good.

The other thing that was different in Manchester than in London was the timings of the exhibition, the hours weren't quite as long to be open and that really did make a difference for us.

The guided tours were not as busy as in London and thankfully we were able to cancel a couple that hadn't been subscribed to. After over 50 guided tours in London in the space of a couple of weeks my voice was really struggling to cope and to be honest as soon as the exhibition was up and running in Manchester I dipped.

Thank God for Alex Lodge. He knew the exhibition inside out and was able to run some of the guided tours for me in Manchester. To be honest I think he ran most of them, especially for that first week.

The gang really clubbed together and took it all on between them and this was a huge relief for me. I had been so run down by everything and had just kept fighting, just kept going because I had to because the minute I gave up, they would give up and absolutely everything would fall apart.

The gang worked hard to get me that opening day off and I was able to go back to the flat relatively early and get my PJs on and chill out.

What a world apart from London. There was no major pressure on us from the venue as we had been managing to make payments to them and other costs in Manchester were minimal. The accommodation had been paid in advance and so it was time to try and get caught up on some other bills. But for now, for today, I passed out on the couch.

I am awful at realising my limitations and hate to admit that I can't do something or that I have to stop. What I never factored in with the exhibition was the fact that only three months ago I'd undergone major surgery to have my thyroid removed. I'd still not gotten used to my new medication and there were moments where I literally struggled to find the energy to lift one leg in front of the other.

I honestly have no idea how I/we had managed to get through the previous couple of weeks but beyond that I have absolutely no idea how I have manged to get through a full half a year running on nothing but empty. How was it August? How had 2018 passed in such a blur?

That afternoon and early evening I sat and had a cry, for everything that had happened in London but not only that but for the first time in over a year I allowed myself to feel sorry for myself. I was wounded and had no idea how to even begin to get myself back on track. For now, pizza, sleep, cuddles and kindness for a few days would certainly help a little.

Again, Alex gave me a bit of a talking to, she had to go home to the boys but before she left she gave me a quick kick up the bum:

> "I get that you need a few days to pick yourself up so take them, let Steven, Alex and Georgia help you, and then get on with it."

One thing I will never regret about the exhibition is Alex Maughan, her loyalty, her will to get things done, her ability to stand up to me and say no, but most of all her friendship. She is one of these people that walks into a room gives you a cheeky smirk and you know it's going to be a good day.

Whilst the venue was nowhere near as intense as London had been, we still had a balance to pay and we had to pay this in instalments to them. There was a couple of tense moments where we maybe missed a payment by a day but Tom Ford the financials guy at Manchester Central was beyond amazing. Handsome in a strange way, and always tried to be as fair as he could and as helpful as he could. Not like in London at all.

The other thing about Manchester was that there were absolutely no hidden charges. No, "oh we need to charge you all this extra for security guards you don't need or that also protect the rest of the building anyway". No, "oh the electricity you are using is more than the Blackpool Illuminations, without warning". All the costs for Manchester were up front and honest and as a result were covered and the exhibition eventually ran at a slight profit.

If we had managed to get a PR campaign going for the Manchester exhibition in even half the capacity that we had for London, then I am pretty sure the exhibition would still be running today. Problem is we couldn't pay the PR company even £1000 because the BDC had eaten up every bit of our funds. Quite rightly the PR company withdrew their services.

Manchester had so much about it, and whilst times were really tough later on in the Manchester journey at the beginning point it gave us the chance to heal, to be away from the sour taste from the Business Design Centre and to start having fun with visitors again.

It wasn't uneventful. There was an ambulance for a little boy who fell and split his head wide open with blood pouring everywhere. The poor soul had tripped over his own feet and smacked his head on the edge of his little brother's pram. The strangest thing ever happened that day. I was doing one of the guided tours and I noticed that something was wrong over to the side of the Viva Forever stage. I went over to investigate, and it was this little boy and his family. I asked some people to clear the area to give them some privacy and asked one of the girls to take charge and make sure everything was ok but... The first thing the dad said to me was

> "Don't worry you are not liable, he tripped and fell and hit the pram."

Is this really how parents feel or how venues feel about these things? I couldn't have cared less if I was liable or not. The only thing that mattered was that the little boy was okay. Not for one second had a thought about a claim or blame cross my mind. Has it really become that bad?

The little boy's parents kept in touch with me after they had been to the hospital and thankfully, he was absolutely fine and back to his usual self within a day or two. His mum had thanked me for my help and concern but said:

"It wouldn't have been as bad if it wasn't his birthday party tomorrow and he fell two weeks ago the day before his nursery pictures."

Oh no the little guy must be a bit accident prone, and his poor mother must have been thinking, what next?

Other than that incident there were not really many disasters from the Manchester Central exhibition. It ran quite smoothly, thanks mostly to Georgia, Alex Lodge and the two boys from Manchester that helped us (Dane and Adam).

What did happen in Manchester were lots of familiar faces visiting, celebrities that had either been in Coronation Street or other TV shows. Marty from Shameless visited one day (you know the guy with the Tourette's tics that is brilliant). I was a little star struck but he was lovely, couldn't have been kinder and really seemed to enjoy the guided tour.

The most exciting thing that happened in Manchester was the visit we had from the two Spice mums. We had no idea that they were coming until we got a little hint from Andrea Brown's Twitter account (Mel B's Mum). She sent out a little tweet saying off to Manchester for a Spicy day out with Joan O'Neil, AKA Mel C's Mum.

I can't remember if I messaged him or him me, but I know we both have tweet notification alerts from Andrea and instantly Alex Lodge and I were in a texting frenzy of are they or aren't they?

I think that was probably the slowest morning I have ever had at the exhibition, sitting biting my nails really nervous about the fact two of the Spice Girls' mums could be on their way to my exhibition.

There was the usual guided tour that day and I wondered maybe if they would come for that but no, the guided tour started and I had to do my very best to keep myself composed and give everyone a good tour, despite the fact my mind was not focussed and racing at a million miles an hour.

I was as excited about the prospect of meeting the Spice Mums as I ever was meeting the girls themselves.

Andrea had followed me on twitter years ago and we had occasional conversations online, nothing major just basic chit chat.

Joan, I had met briefly at a Melanie C gig just a month before at Boisdale Café in London.

I had given everyone a brief about being nice to them but not overly fussing and making them feel uncomfortable. Briefing them just on the chance that they might be on their way.

By the time I came out of the exhibition an hour and a half later I was starting to think that they maybe weren't coming to the exhibition.

Walking out the door to the exhibition hall, I was still chatting to the people on the guided tour, and Georgia gave me the thumbs up and a big cheesy grin that told me the mother ships had landed. I was beyond excited and whilst I didn't want to be rude to anyone on the tour I was absolutely dying to go and meet Andrea in person and thank her for her support and kind words online.

They had just arrived and just gone into the start of the exhibition, I took the chance to go and say hello and introduce myself.

Just as I had imagined, they couldn't have been nicer and were so down to earth with me. Joan and Andrea were both a little bit emotional. I asked them if they wanted a tour or if they were happy to have a nosey around, they chose to have a nosey and so I thanked them for coming and said that I hoped they enjoyed the trip down memory lane and that hopefully we could chat a little bit at the end.

My heart was racing as I stood there talking to two of the ladies that had given us our Melanies, Sporty and Scary, two of my favourite ladies in the whole world, two of the most iconic ladies in the world and here is me as a fan, asking if they wanted me to show them around. It was easily the best moment of the Manchester exhibitions.

There had been a little boy on the guided tour called Lucian. Lucian had wanted to come to the exhibition in London, but his mum had got the dates wrong and they missed it. To make it up to him, she had brought him up to Manchester for the day to see the exhibition there and have a day out together.

Lucian knew everything there was to know about the Spice Girls and spent the tour asking me all sorts of interesting questions, really putting me on the spot and putting my Spice Girls knowledge to the test. To be honest it enhanced the experience for everyone else, it was nice to have someone else to bounce info and facts off.

We got to the 'Stop' section and Lucian was right there with his hand up dying to ask a question:

> "Stop was the Spice Girls' first single release that didn't make it to number 1, but what was the song that beat it to number one?"

Oh my God, I'm stumped, I know the answer, I've always known the answer but right at this moment in time I had absolutely no idea, neither did he but it gave us a great discussion point and I assured him I would Google it at my first opportunity.

It was in fact Run DMC "It's Like That" that kept the Spice Girls from number one. I know this not because I remembered to go and Google it after, but because a week later I got an amazing email from young 10-year-old Lucian to tell me he had found out and he wanted to let me know the answer. This made my day and to be honest it is moments like this that I will remember forever. I won't concentrate on the negativity but purely on the fact that in some way, the exhibition had a big enough impact on this little guy that he had wanted to take the time to send me an email. What a little superstar!

Anyway, back to the story, Lucian had been on the tour and I had seen just how enthusiastic he had been about the Spice Girls and how much he knew about them. I couldn't resist telling him that the Spice Mums were in the exhibition and when I saw how excited he was I offered to introduce him.

Lucian was actually a really shy, quiet boy and despite the fact he had been outgoing asking me questions, he really retracted into himself and was terribly star struck when meeting the two mums.

I introduced him to Andrea first and she was really lovely to him. I tried to get him chatting a little, but he really couldn't get his words out and we moved on to say a quick hello to Joany as well. Both mums were so kind in their time with Lucian and I think it really made his day, I know it made my day.

It made my whole week! In fact, it really was one of the highlights of the whole exhibition experience, I say that a lot, but it really was all an incredible privilege. Getting to have a chat with the girls' families is a privilege. It must come with its own intrusions and difficulties and at the end of the day whilst they are mega superstars, even the girls themselves are just human.

Once the mums had spent about an hour in the exhibition they came back out and were happy to stand and chat to us and get pictures taken with us. They couldn't have been nicer and were telling us loads of things about the girls growing up and their experiences.

It was so interesting to hear the stories and again I felt like it was such a privilege to be listening to the mums chatting about the girls' achievements. Both were obviously incredibly proud of their girls and they were quite happy to chat about it.

Andrea tells about the girls being on tour, reels off the exact number of shows the girls have performed and says quite proudly:

> "They never missed or cancelled one single show. I remember Melanie being ill, really sick, phoning Simon and begging him to get her a doctor. She still went on stage that night. I don't know how she did it, but she was up there."

It was amazing to hear the tales direct from them, not through a tabloid or from a friend of a friend but from the mums of my heroes.

I chatted about gigging with Joan and she had mentioned seeing me at a few of Melanie's gigs, and also chatted about her still gigging and what she had coming up herself. She was telling me she still has one of the Aprilia mopeds at her house along with a few other bits and bobs.

They left the exhibition and headed for lunch at China town in Manchester, the feedback was positive, and I was on a massive high from their visit.

The other thing that sticks in my mind the most

about Manchester was having to start ignoring my phone a little bit. People were chasing for money and you will know if you have ever been in debt to a company they do not give up when you are any kind of payment behind.

With the London venue taking every penny we had it was taking us more time than people wanted to allow us to get our finances in order and very quickly demands starting to come in for payments and the people were phoning and phoning and phoning and phoning.

It was a change, I normally couldn't get to calls for being on other calls and people had been complaining that they could never get through to me. Now, here I was unable to face another phone call asking about payments, unable to answer the phone and listen to another company threatening me with all sorts.

It was all so bittersweet. I was proud that we had managed to get the exhibition from London at all never mind set up and running in a second venue halfway up the country in Manchester. I was proud that it was working out and people were coming and then so unbelievably worried and stressed about all this bloody money we still owed out and had to try and get paid back.

In amongst all of this I had noticed Steven had changed a little. He had become quiet, withdrawn and his face constantly had this pained expression on it. He knew we had worked harder than ever before, but yet here we were in Manchester, hundreds of thousands of pounds owed out. We had to make it work, we had to keep it going if there was any chance at all.

21

Out of Your Mind

Steven had to leave Manchester after only a few days. He had his full-time job to go back to and of course there are only so many holidays that he could take to help me out. So, for the first time with the exhibition we were living apart. I was in Manchester and Steven was back down in London.

Being apart was so hard on us both, it doesn't matter what the world throws at us, as long as we are together Steven and I can deal with it and work our way through it. Being apart, we were both struggling, and it wasn't just me that was getting the hounding phone calls, Steven's phone was ringing off the hook as well.

I was still living in the rented flat, but we only had that for a limited time, and I would have to move on from it at some point, but where to?

There was another burning issue with the exhibition at this point. The exhibition was turning a small profit in Manchester and it was helping us a little bit, nowhere near where we wanted it to be. However, it was still better than nothing and we knew the only way the business was going to have a chance at all was to extend the run in Manchester.

Manchester Central wasn't available and had bookings due to arrive the day after we were due to close, we couldn't even extend it by a couple of days there.

Don't get me wrong we had been having some amazing talks in the background about future exhibitions: Birmingham, Glasgow, Liverpool, Watford and a few others but they were not immediate and unless the exhibition stayed open and kept creating a revenue then we could not keep servicing the payments we owed. The minute it closed there was no income and absolutely no chance of making it to a future exhibition in Birmingham or indeed anywhere else.

Nobody else could do it so it was down to me to start frantically sending out emails and making phone calls to local Manchester venues. Every venue that I could possibly find in Manchester that could possibly host the exhibition got an email from us.

Not only were we looking for a venue, but we were looking for somewhere for free or as close to free as possible. It seemed like an impossible task but as usual I refuse to give up until I absolutely have to. Not only that but I believed in this exhibition more than anything and I would have done anything I needed to take make it work.

We were lucky in a way, that the shopping centre next door, The Great Northern Warehouse had a space that we could use. They tried to charge us £5k a month rent for it but after a week in it I knew it wasn't even worth £500 a month rent.

The Manchester Central exhibition had one design flaw to it and that was that it only ran for 12 days. We couldn't get the venue longer, but we really wanted to go to Manchester straight after London and so we took it.

Now, however, we were scratching around trying to find every penny that we could and every avenue open to us to keep going. Anything we could just to keep the cash flow going and give us a chance of being able to pay people back.

There were so many bonuses to moving it just next door, not only the logistics of it being so close but also it was still in the exact area that we had started to become familiar with and felt secure with.

There was one major drawback for me at this stage. I didn't realise this was a kind of Manchester vibe, but the Great Northern Warehouse was exactly what it said on the tin - a warehouse. The space was at best rustic and at worst just a building site.

For the first time with the exhibition I really struggled to see how it was going to work. This wasn't what I wanted for my amazing exhibition. It was meant to be polished, crisp and clean. This was dusty, concrete and iron. There was no real lighting to speak of other than awful floodlights, but what choice did we have? It was this or close forever and at least this way we would buy ourselves some more time to get some decent venues and sponsorships sorted.

We were always working with people in the background and right up until the day the exhibition actually closed down, people always believed in it and wanted to be involved with it. We had a new sponsorship company called BDS and they were so sure they could get us a tour of venues with amazing sponsorship. I still had to believe and still had to push forward.

The one thing the Great Northern Warehouse could do for us, despite the fact I didn't like it, was to buy us time and with no additional overheads and with the costs now negotiated even lower we were again hoping that the steady stream of visitors would help us make in-roads into the debt whilst we secured the tour.

We could make the exhibition work in the industrial space, but I knew I had to sit down, be clever about it and make the most of the much smaller much more rustic space that we had to play with. I also had to do it quickly as time was fast running out at Manchester Central and if we couldn't make it work, we would have to get it home.

With some clever coloured mood lighting, a roaming spotlight or two and some equally industrial partition walls we were able to create something that resembled the exhibition that we had known. Of course, we had all the signs and reading materials, but we had to pull out every trick that we had, all the posters, the rare signs, the cardboard cut outs. Anything we could just to cover the industrial walls.

I shouldn't have bothered, with it being Manchester, I didn't know, but people are used to the industrial rustic vibe and in fact the more I stayed in the city the more I realised it. The people that came to the exhibition there loved it for its traditional Manchester vibe. I never got used to it and it was easily my least favourite of all the exhibitions. It was different and I'm glad we did it, we had to, but it wasn't up to the same standard as the others had been.

The biggest pain about the Great Northern Warehouse was the fact that you couldn't walk over a short bridge between venues holding the items. They had to be packed into a van, unpacked at the loading bay and then taken up the venue space through an industrial loading lift. It was a nightmare, beyond a nightmare but again it had to be done, it was either move it or close for good.

Again, it was a massive task to try and move it and get it up and sorted in the new venue. It seemed like a never-ending task this time, Alex Lodge was back for a day or two, Steven was back and of course Georgia AKA the machine was also there. Between us we managed to get it up and ready to open within a couple of days but again it broke us.

It broke us all physically, it's not easy moving hundreds of staging, mannequins, walls and everything else that goes with it. It is incredibly physically demanding and against the clock the pressure of getting it done on time really does make it harder.

Georgia absolutely broke her back for us these couple of days, working from 9am in the morning until 11pm one day. That day I knew Georgia wasn't happy about it, wasn't happy about the hours, the level of pressure and the aching bones and exhaustion that went with it.

We had a chat about this after and from then I was more aware that whilst this was my project and I was incredibly passionate about it, I was asking too much of the people that were keeping the exhibition together, keeping me together and it had to slow down.

It did slow down, in fact it slowed down way too much. By the time we had moved to the Great Northern Warehouse we immediately lost footfall in comparison to Manchester Central. It was natural, there was nowhere near the same amount of awareness.

However, we had been assured that the Great Northern Warehouse was a thriving entertainments centre and that it was the perfect place for us to showcase the exhibition. The truth of it was there was about five people a day walking through the shopping centre (that's not really too much of an exaggeration either for weekdays). The weekends were a bit better but during the week there was literally nobody in the centre and after two weeks of being there we were averaging around 20 customers a day.

The exhibition at the Great Northern Warehouse was meant to extend right up until Christmas but we had to take a break for a few days around 15th October for a pre-booked event. At this point we had to dismantle the exhibition for the event and then put it back together.

It was as we approached this date that I realised it was just not viable and we simply didn't have the manpower, the energy, or the resources to pull it apart and put it back together again in the same week. With the customer levels dropping every day it came to the point in Manchester where I had to make the decision to close.

The final decision came when intu Watford agreed to have us on the run up to Christmas in what they were telling us was one of the top 20 shopping centres in the UK. With this in the pipeline I hoped that despite the dire financial situation we were in, at least there was something booked and something we could work towards.

For now, we needed time out, we had the shit kicked out of us both physically and emotionally for months now and we needed some time to get our head around the situation, some time hopefully to get some kind of rescue bid in place.

The Great Northern Warehouse went from trying to charge us £5k a month to £5k for the whole rental period up until Christmas in a bid to get us to stay. But it wouldn't have mattered if it had been for free as there was no way we could have made the numbers work. They knew it was bogus and they had been desperate at times to have us in the space, but no venue just slashes the rent costs, willing to offer months and months of rent for the original price of one month. They were absolutely taking the piss, the venue was totally failing, I hope they manage to make it work in the long term, but we were not their answer.

Sitting there day in and day out with nobody coming into the exhibition for hours on end but having to be there because there were maybe 10 advance tickets booked, we couldn't shorten hours any further and we couldn't let people down by not being open.

I couldn't have done this without Georgia! Georgia kept me going, she was my confidante, my friend and I trusted her with absolutely everything. Not only that but Georgia has a really positive outlook and a very intelligent opinion to offer.

The other issue I was constantly having to deal with in Manchester was accommodation. It got tougher and tougher to afford somewhere to live, with the bank accounts empty and every penny we had going straight back out to try and pay some debt off it literally got to a stage in Manchester where I had a room booked for the weekend but come Monday there was nothing in place and no money to book another flat for a week.

Eventually I was down to booking the cheapest room I could find for a night at a time and I knew that it just couldn't go on. I had actually considered bedding down in the exhibition. That was madness given it was a freezing cold warehouse, but at one point that's how skint we were. That's how close it came to total utter disaster.

As it got closer and closer to the date, we had to pull the exhibition down for a few days I realised It just wasn't viable. It wasn't working in terms of numbers and the bus, which was now parked outside, was just being targeted rather than enjoyed.

The bus also had to be moved for a couple of weekend markets and the cost of doing that was crazy. The visitor numbers were down, it was torture sitting there day in day out with nobody coming to the exhibition, and at all times there had to be at least two people working.

Having heard from intu Watford that they wanted us in December, knowing that now we were losing money by staying open, and with no money in the bank it was getting harder and harder to afford accommodation.

The decision had to be made and we had to stop. We

quite simply weren't able to tear it down and build it back up and then hope that we could somehow turn our fortunes around. The flow of people through the centre was dire, there was no way we could turn it around.

22

Stop Right Now

After the decision was made to stop and retreat, we had to put the plan into action and try and get enough manpower together to get the whole exhibition away from the venue and back down to London.

It's funny when you are on your way up, everyone wants to be involved, everyone wants to help you out and enjoy the ride, but when you are on your way down and on the absolute bones of your arse, all of a sudden everyone is busy or has prior plans.

Pulling that exhibition down in Manchester and getting it back to our house in London was the hardest thing I have ever had to do and by the end of it we were all completely broken.

My husband Steven is a machine sometimes and when he puts his mind to something, the level of determination he shows I have never seen from any other man in my entire life!

Josh calls him 'Ant Man', he can lift so much on his back, like a pack horse, he really is unbelievable.

Packing up the exhibition for the first day was

Georgia, Ruby and Hannah (who were all having to be paid) and Steven. We packed up all the excess equipment, mannequins, boxes etc. that hadn't been used in Manchester. The heaviest part of it was the partition walls and it took at least two of us to move them to the van, the problem was once it was packed into the van poor Steven had to drive down to London from Manchester and then unload the full van on his own. I had to stay in Manchester. Steven single-handedly unloaded the full van, floor to roof, on his own, shifting panels, motorbikes and all sorts.

The real problem was, that as soon as he was unpacked in London he had to turn around and come straight back to Manchester for the next run. Steven did this for a full five days in a row and even had to go to work and put in a shift a few of those days. I don't know how or where he got the energy from.

Gone was the logistics company that had a team of men helping us out, the exhibition was so big it literally took a team of twenty men to move it from London to Manchester along with at least six vans. Yet here we were with one single van and absolutely no manpower in comparison. We had no idea how we were going to do it, but it had to be done.

The one thing that we did have for now, was a place to put it all, it would be a tight squeeze with every corner of the place full to the top, but given we had a huge basement and attic it could all just about fit into our own house. It wasn't much fun living with it all around us, piled high in boxes, tripping over everything from boxes of dolls to platform shoes.

Georgia once again absolutely broke her back to help us get the job done, sweating, and for the first time ever having a little moan about how much pressure it was. Georgia is my guardian angel, she got me through Manchester and her crazy silliness is beyond infectious. She makes me want to be a healthier, more educated and more tolerant person. It's simple, without Georgia there would have been no Manchester exhibitions, she is Miss Manchester Spice.

That last few days, I was staying in a grotty hotel that was used by the council as an overspill hostel. It stank of fags, booze and sick and everyone in the place was out of their face. I smoke and drink, so for me to say it stank of fags, you can get the extent of it.

On that last day in Manchester, it took us absolutely forever to get the last of it done. It seemed to go on and on, probably because we were all running on empty, but it really did feel like forever to get it finished.

We ended up having to leave some mannequins behind along with a couple of other boxes of aids. The van was full and there was no way we were getting one single other item into it. It was 10.30pm at least by the time we got the van packed and with a five-hour drive ahead of us it was going to be a harsh trip.

We left Georgia in Manchester, her choice as she wanted to explore the city a bit more before leaving. Josh and I set off from Manchester, me driving (Steven had to be in work), and the two of us were absolutely physically broken.

I got cramp in my legs about five times on the journey home and Josh wasn't much good, he was sleeping just half an hour into the drive and woke briefly at the service station.

The weather was absolutely shit and I am the most nervous driver ever. I was in a massive crash on the motorway with a lorry years ago and it really affected my confidence driving on the motorway.

The high sided van and the high winds really made it a tense drive and only half an hour into the drive my neck and shoulders were already sore from being so tense. The winds would blow the van from side to side and every so often I would wake Josh up shouting 'Fuck' as the van hurtled to the side with another huge gust. It felt like mother nature was telling me to stop, either that or punish me for getting it so bloody wrong.

We eventually got home around 4am that morning and the sun was coming up by the time I got to sleep. We couldn't unpack the last van load at that time in the morning, so it had to wait until the next day. Josh was straight off to bed and being so relieved to be home it literally took me hours to come down from the drive.

A drive that nearly didn't happen, after doing five trips in the van previously we had used hundreds of pounds worth of diesel and we were down to our very last pennies. We didn't even have enough money to fill the van for the last run and if it hadn't been for my mum and dad lending me some money, we wouldn't have got it all home. It took a lot to ask for that money as I wasn't on great terms with my dad.

Nevertheless, I had managed to get the entire collection home to London, packed into my house with every single space full of some kind of exhibition memorabilia, whether it was mannequins, staging or costumes, it was absolutely everywhere. I was worried about the floor of the basement falling through under the weight of all the staging, mannequins and barriers stacked to the ceiling on it. The floor genuinely dipped in the middle. The same happened when we put it into a storage unit, the lock on the door didn't match up because the weight on the floor had made the door frame dip down.

Getting home was strange. Having all the stuff around me was torture. It felt like there was nowhere I could go that wasn't overflowing with Spice Girls' stuff. It was like a nightmare maze that you can never find your way out of. Not only was it my collection and all the staging but it was all the other collections and clothing as well that belonged to the other collectors and designers.

I was numb. I was broken. I was exhausted. I was

financially broke. I was stressed, so so stressed, anxious and most of all, worried about Steven and how the fuck we were going to get ourselves out of this mess.

I couldn't do anything; I couldn't sort out the boxes or the collection. I struggled to physically move for the first few days after it, my bones ached, my muscles ached and I was in total shock, totally lost with no idea where to even begin picking up the pieces. All I needed was cuddles with my beautiful beagle doggies and my husband. I couldn't sleep, it didn't matter how hard I tried my mind just wouldn't switch off. I'd been the same in Manchester, especially sleeping on my own, I was getting maybe four hours sleep a night and then I'd be horrendously tired for the rest of the day.

Already at this point I was selling off parts of the collection, doubles of CDs that I had or rare one offs that wouldn't necessarily make a massive difference to the exhibition if we managed to keep it going.

It broke my heart selling any of the collection, these are all items that I have collected individually. If I think carefully most of them have an individual story to them, to their purchase and history. It doesn't matter whether it is a CD, a doll or a costume, I always like to know where they are coming from and who has owned them. It is part of the whole story. That story of the collection is one that nobody will ever know but me. It's unique. I couldn't ever possibly write it all down in a book, there were thousands of items and as I looked at every single one of them, I could feel its history, tell where it had come from, somehow remember stupid details about almost every single item in the collection. The Victoria Beckham-style icon dress came from a fan who was sick and had to pay medical bills. I gave them the fairest price I could rather than trying to get it cheap. I've done this with all the items, they are worth what they are worth, I've never traded in misery.

As far as the public and everyone else was concerned, even at this point, everything was fine, and we were looking forward to a new exhibition. The heartache, the stress, the constant chasing phone calls for money, they were all hidden away. That wasn't what people could see of us if we had any chance of making it work, and we still couldn't give up.

We couldn't keep going on like this, and so we had to write to all of our creditors and tell them about the situation we were facing. It was tough to admit we had struggled to make a profit or even a break even situation, but pride comes before a fall and we needed one last chance to try and make it work, one last chance to prove that actually it could be a very successful business model.

We had invested so much money in staging and mannequins and everything else that it was tough to see that it wasn't going to work out. Maybe we should have given up at this point. Looking back in hindsight this probably should have been the end of it. This should have been the point where we realised, it didn't matter how much work we put in, it didn't matter how much we were willing to break ourselves physically to get the job done. The great big black hole created by the failure in sponsorship and the £60,000 of hidden and additional costs from London had sealed our fate.

We couldn't though, we couldn't give in and there was always this chance of the next opportunity for us. Since splitting with Slingshot Sponsorship, we had been working with a company called BDS Sponsorship. Richard the CEO was an older gentleman and had a little bit of crazy about him, but he also seemed to have a clear game plan and some serious contacts.

He put us in touch with intu Shopping Centres who had centres up and down the country and they were absolutely massive. They were offering us a tour if we could make it work in Geri's hometown of Watford. Let's try it out in a shopping centre and from that we would take it on a tour of shopping centres up and down the country. Truthfully this could have worked. It could have worked if there had been a marketing budget or indeed any level of support or marketing from intu themselves.

Not only did Richard put us in touch with the largest chain of shopping centres in the UK but he had also put us in touch with Birmingham NEC who were uber keen to host the exhibition and also talked of a tour around their venues and other venues that they worked with. Overseas contacts and major players such as the new V & A in Dundee were all looking at scheduling.

Everyone was interested in the exhibition, but nobody was willing to take that financial punt on it.

The other obstacle was me. I was broken and I didn't know if I could do it again. I didn't know if I could go and run an exhibition every day, if I could face the public again knowing what was going on and putting a brave face on it. What was the alternative? Stop? Give up and admit the dream was over?

At this stage the two biggest hurdles were finances and me.

I was down and out and didn't know how to pick myself back up again. I didn't know how to get my head around it all and even put one foot in front of the other or even how to move things around in the house and sort the collection out from the disorganised chaos that it was.

Stop, sleep, talk, cry, fret, scream, don't sleep, pace, worry, cry, and so on....

23

Let Love Lead the Way

When you are at a real low point, remember I had reached my rock bottom only 18 months before now, this wasn't my rock bottom, it was really bloody hard to deal with but given the past 18 months, this was just a situation. One that maybe we could fight our way out of. I had been winded, but you can never keep a good man from fighting back, especially not when he has the amazing friends around him that I do.

Alex Maughan was beyond nervous, she knew the situation and knew in theory that it was over, but it didn't stop her from giving me a virtual kick up the arse through Facetime. Alex Lodge is Spice Girls until he dies and is the most loyal friend in the world. He always has my back and was always encouraging me to fight on.

Maybe we did have a chance. If we stopped and admitted it was over then there was absolutely no chance, and we had to admit that we owed all of this money and couldn't pay it back. This way we had a chance to make it work and pay itself off. The biggest chain of shopping centres wanted us and the first one that we had was Geri's hometown, it had to at least be worth a shot. Of course, it was worth a shot.

The new sponsorship company that we had involved were coming up with ideas and contacts for us all the time. intu shopping centres was a great contact, they have 16 huge shopping centres and if it was successful in Watford, we were looking at a deal for 12 shopping centres in 12 months. That itself took us up to the other proposal on the table from Birmingham NEC.

The deal with intu at Watford was a collaboration and a share in revenue, this helped us to have prime retail space but at the lowest possible costs. On top of that, a collaboration was what we needed, shared costs, joint marketing, joint resources and contacts. There were loads of benefits from it, except one. We were now working with a huge company and just to get permission to fart on the premises was a two-week process.

They weren't experienced in pop-up exhibitions or events and they were hopeless at trying to get anything organised or signed off. When I turned up to look at the unit, I met with some 20-year-old boy who couldn't find the right keys, didn't know where the light switches were or indeed his arse from his elbow.

The lighting in the unit was the only real bonus for us, there were already at least 200 spotlights wired to the roof, so we knew we could at least make the lighting in Watford amazing. Along with the mood lights we had bought for Manchester and the roll up banners we had, making the exhibition look pleasing was the most important thing and we could do that at least.

Everything was a hassle though. The lights had to be tested, the fire alarm had to be tested, the fire exit was broken and needed fixing, the sprinkler system needed to be checked. We had just been handed keys to a unit and then told that all of this was now our responsibility, or we couldn't open. This was the first threat of us not opening. It was just one of around 100 times intu at Watford used the phrase 'you can't open'. I think they were a bit shocked when I told them to shove it up their arses and that we wouldn't be opening. There was no way I was paying out thousands of pounds to have a sprinkler system checked that A, I have never been part of installing and that B, that only needs checked every five years and I will be using for a month. No way.

The fire door was another laugh. The people who had been in the shop before me 'New Look' had broken the fire escape door. Now it was our responsibility to make sure it was in working order. Eh, how about jog on.

Most of the general staff at intu were lovely and we had some really nice security guards that would always stop for a chat on their way past, or the little cleaning lady that would say good morning every day. There was one woman that I clashed with right from the start. To be honest it wasn't me that clashed with her first, it was Alex Maughan and my mum.

I think her name was Vicky, but I am not too sure, our lives were so chaotic at this point that names are the last thing on your mind. Getting through the day was all we were doing by this point.

Getting the stuff in to the shopping centre was a hassle in itself with a loading bay, stinking industrial lift and then a huge corridor up to the back of the unit. Each trolley load that we took, and there was a lot of them given the size of the exhibition, took around ten minutes to get into the unit.

Of course, there was no team of 20 guys helping us, it was Steven, me and sometimes Josh, sometimes Alex Lodge and the gorgeous Alan Chalmers travelled all the way down from Newcastle to help one day. He got on a bus for seven hours over night and then helped us to move the exhibition stuff, not only that but he broke his back doing it and was like a pack horse. He then travelled back another seven hours on the bus to Newcastle. It's moments of kindness like this that will always be what we remember from the whole experience. I've met this guy twice in my life before this and we only really got to know each other through social media and here he is doing a 14-hour trip as well as a full day's graft just to help me out. Friends like Alan are like gold dust, they come along a couple of times in your life if you are lucky. You're amazing Alan Chalmers!

Before we could even build the exhibition, we had to whitewash most of the walls in the unit. New Look had stripped out all the shop fitting units to reveal half wallpapered walls, bare gyprock and electrical wires hanging out all over the place.

Alex Lodge and I spent a day and a half whitewashing the walls whilst Steven and Josh built some of the staging around us. By the time we got to the second coat of paint Steven was able to follow us around slotting parts of the staging into place as we went along.

I keep saying it was hard going and it was, but this woman Vicky was really starting to get right on my fucking nerves! We had been in for five days absolutely working our asses off in trying with every single bit of energy that any of us had left just to get the exhibition built up and along comes fucking Vicky and her equally fucking rude Health & Safety twat colleague.

> "You need to replace the roof tiles that are missing or you are not opening."

> "You need to fix the back door or you are not opening."

> "There is a bit of cellotape on the front window you need to move or you are not opening." (what, the same bit of cellotape that has been there for the past four months since the first time I visited the centre?!)

"You need to fix the hand dryer in the staff toilet or you are not opening!"

On top of this Vicky had said something to piss Alex off majorly. I can't remember what it was, but then she made her last mistake, she pissed my mum off, offended my mum and was just rude.

"RIGHT VICKY FUCK OFF, OUT THE SHOP!!!"

I couldn't have cared less if she was the centre manager or the Queen of England, when my PA who has been like my right hand for two years and more importantly my mother is offended, you can fuck right off. I picked up the phone to the Managing Director and told him I would rather walk away from the whole thing than work in these conditions with some jumped up fucking idiot threatening to close us down or stop us from opening every two minutes, and now she offended my mum so I am offended by her behaviour.

I'm sure Jens got straight on the phone to Vicky as she was back down at the shop trying to apologise within five minutes claiming that we have just got off on the wrong foot. Yes Vicky we were stressed out our boxes, trying everything we could to make everything work on absolutely no budget and here you were asking us to fix problems and issues at a cost to us, that we had absolutely nothing to do with or responsibility for and being incredible rude in the process.

As you can probably tell, my tolerance for idiots at this point was at an all-time low. I am for the most part quite a patient person and I like to think I always give people a fair chance. Unfortunately, that would not be the last time that Vicky and I clashed.

The day arrived for us to open the exhibition and I have to say that again whilst it was awesome it wasn't quite what I had hoped for from it. We had managed to make the space work as best we could with a clear path around, but it was now in a shop unit rather than an exhibition hall, so it wasn't my favourite look.

What was my favourite was how we opened the Watford exhibition. Every other time it had been a launch evening with Spice Girls' cocktails, music etc but this time it was a morning opening and we had very special little guest called Oliver to open it for us.

Oliver had visited the first exhibition in London, he was 10 years old and was a massive Spice Girls and Little Mix fan. He was wearing a Little Mix t-shirt and had a Spice Girls' phone cover the first time I met him, and he was such a delight to chat to.

Oliver has some hassles sometimes in school and is on the autism spectrum, something I have a lot of experience with. To see him coming to the exhibition and enjoying himself really made everything worthwhile. There was nobody better that I could think of to open the exhibition for us than Oliver. I had asked his mum if it would be possible for him to cut the ribbon and since it was a Friday morning, he would have to get the morning off school.

Not only did Oliver get the day off school but his school had decided to make a big thing of it for him, inviting him to do some writing about it and mentioning it in their newsletter. I don't know if it's helped little Oliver, but I am always delighted when I get updates from his mum or from him on Instagram telling me what the latest addition to his collection is.

The day that Oliver opened the exhibition and cut the ribbon for us, I could tell he was a little bit nervous and shy about it. However, he ploughed ahead and did a fantastic job of it. Afterwards I gave him a little box of Spice Girls' items that I maybe had doubles of or could live without, I've never seen anyone so happy and he was all emotional running back to his mum. Oliver, buddy, you and a few other young people I met in the journey of the exhibition have made every bit of it worthwhile. Follow your heart buddy, be you, be unique but most of all have lots of fun doing it. I expect to hear about your Spice Girls' collection breaking records in the future!

We knew that advanced ticket sales for Watford were not on the same scale as London or either of the Manchester exhibitions, but we had been assured that we were in one of the busiest shopping centres in the UK and with it leading up to Christmas, it would be crazy busy.

Again, there was no budget for any major marketing campaigns or PR. We had tried to get local radio stations involved with competitions and the same with local newspapers, all things that we were assured we would get help with as intu has contacts with these people, even active accounts with them. No, we were on or own and unless we were willing to spend thousands on advertising none of the local rags wanted to touch it. It was coming up to Christmas and they could fill pages and pages of adverts for toys etc.

We chased intu to put adverts up on their digital display boards, at their information centre, as well an email drop, posts on their social media channels, everything that we could.

What we got from them was a trade style press release the day before we were due to open, it was weeks late, nobody could get their act together and my feedback about the press release was that I didn't even finish reading it, I didn't finish reading it and it was about my bloody exhibition. It was single-handedly the dullest thing I have ever read in my life and quite clearly whoever wrote it has never had to write a press release for mainstream media before.

As soon as I got the email, I was on the phone to the Managing Director saying that under no circumstances was this press release ever to go out about the exhibition at Watford. It would do more damage than good and was not how I wanted the fun, feel-good exhibition to be represented. Dull, boring, drab, unreadable and full of irrelevant information about how many parking spaces there were or what the anticipated footfall of the centre was. For fuck's sake guys we are selling a Girl Power exhibition, not 'how to make yourself bored and suicidal' guide.

So, here we are, little Oliver has done a grand job of opening the exhibition for us and it's now our first full day open. Twenty tickets booked, it was not a worry, we are now in one of the biggest and busiest shopping centres in the UK.... So where are the people?

By the time we closed the exhibition later that night we had a grand total of around thirty people through the door all day and here we were again. Everyone was really interested in what we were doing and saying they would come back with their Christmas office party or with their friends but the traffic actually walking past the shop was non-existent. There were points where we could sit at the front desk and not see one other person in sight.

To top it all off we still had a list of things that Vicky had been moaning to us about and we needed to get them sorted, even if it was just to get her off our backs and out of our faces.

The next day, after working most of the night to get the exhibition sorted out and up to scratch especially the shop windows, Vicky came down to the shop bringing with her four of her colleagues. They stood at our still unfinished shop window, pointing, shaking their heads and pursing their faces.

"Alan, can I just have a quick word?"

Vicky had come over with her back up to where I was sitting with my mum and Alex.

"Not fucking really I'm busy Vicky."

I don't know what kind of response she was hoping for, but I really wasn't in the mood and judging by the fact she had brought four others along with her, she wasn't here for just a friendly chat.

> "I can't let you stay open with the windows like this Alan, we have all agreed, that this, this and this needs to change and we are going to have to ask you to close until you fix it."

It was stupid things like the fake snow not being even or the bloody bit of cellotape left from New Look that I kept forgetting to remove.

> "Fine just close us, but I won't be opening it back up. If I have to turn customers away today for these tiny little nit-picks that you have been walking past every day for the past four months at least, that are actually nothing to do with me, fuck you Vicky, I'm not opening back up."

I am sure Vicky thought that having her back up with her, and with the fact we were in the middle of the shopping centre would be enough for her to walk all over me. Not so.

Every time Vicky thought it was okay to raise her voice I just raised mine louder, anytime she swore under her breath or said she didn't care, I swore out loud and told her to fuck off, until at one point one of her colleagues pointed out to her that she was having a screaming match in the middle of the centre.

"Can we take this inside Alan?"

"No can we fuck, you have said what you think so I will just go and close the shop now."

I headed straight over to the shop keys and started to bring the front shutter down. Fuck it, I've had enough. I've done nothing but work 24-hour days, break myself physically, financially, emotionally. I've watched my husband age ten years in three months, and you are moaning about a bit of fucking cellotape I didn't even put there and threatening to close me.

Let me do it for you.

I couldn't close the shutter fully as there was a couple of people in at the time. My blood was absolutely boiling, everything we were going through trying to fight with everything we had just to give us one last chance, and this rude woman is just jumping right on my last nerve.

I had to walk away from the exhibition, go for a cigarette and a walk around the town whilst deciding what was going to happen now. My mum and Alex were sitting a bit worried thinking I might have actually finally lost the plot.

Not long had I stepped outside when I had Jens on the phone.

> "Alan, please don't do this, the guys are just not used to having a pop-up kind of event in the shopping centre and are not realising they have to be a little bit more flexible."

Well it's not my bloody job to tell them mate and I had enough on my plate without having to deal with your halfwit centre manager with a God complex. Jens couldn't have been nicer and it wasn't long until Vicky was back again with her tail between her legs.

Sorry that they had been so on our backs, they just have the best interest of the centre at heart and they have very high standards for it….. blah blah blah. What really made me laugh was Vicky standing saying:

> "You know I really think me and you could be really good friends and that we have just got off on the wrong foot"

No Vicky you are wrong, I don't think we ever could be friends, my friends all have at least basic manners and conversational skills. I don't know what your issue was, whether it was because I trashed the press release or whatever else, but my suggestion is go get a shag and stop taking shit so seriously.

With Vicky to the side, the day-to-day running of the

exhibition was back to being incredibly tedious. We were sitting there for ten hours a day for maybe 20 people to come into the exhibition. We kept being reassured that the centre would get busier but here we are on our last chance with very few customers actually coming in the door.

No PR. No support from the venue or local press. No advertising budget. We had hoped that the supposed huge footfall of intu would be what helped us get the word out there. Not only that but the day we opened was also the day of the Christmas lights switch on and we had been promised a massive event with a celebrity launch and special mentions about the exhibition to the expected 50,000 crowd.

None and I mean absolutely none of the above happened, the centre wouldn't even allow us to put up an A4 poster without paying £200 for the privilege. What happened to the collaboration? The joint effort?

Maybe I ruffled a few feathers up the wrong way. I was exhausted and a little less patient than normal, but I am still me, and the lack of support or interaction from a company we were meant to be in partnership with was beyond shocking.

The phone was ringing off the hook with people chasing us for loan repayments, or outstanding invoices or for one thing or another. We had tried to keep up with everything we could and were always hoping that our fortunes could turn.

We didn't actually need that much to survive as a company, we needed about 1,000 people per week through the doors of the Watford exhibition and that would allow us to service the debts, keep people happy and keep building on the tour.

With nobody coming though, time was running out and our last chance very quickly became a reality that it was not going to work. That without significant PR there was no way we could keep the exhibition going.

We had talked about it a couple of times but now it really was time to go and get some good legal advice and find out the process of liquidating the company. Neither Steven or I knew much about the process or even how to start it off and as with everything else it started with a Google search.

The hardest thing I have ever had to do was admit to myself that it was over, that the dream of taking the exhibition all around the world wasn't going to happen. It was never about getting rich quick. We had already put years of work in, but it was about doing it for a living and having the experiences that it brought with it.

It wasn't to be and despite all of our hard work and efforts, after giving it absolutely every single ounce of energy that we had, it wasn't working and now we were going to lose it all.

24

The Bailiffs are Calling

The phone calls really were constant, four calls a day from Barclaycard, four calls a day from my bank, four calls a day minimum from Amigo Loans, four calls a day from someone else, ten emails an hour and so on. That wears you down and is very very stressful to deal with. People really don't want to hear that you don't have any money to pay them and why would they be happy with that?

We had arranged a meeting with a liquidation company who were able to give us some free advice on a consultation basis.

I presumed I was going bankrupt, that the company was bankrupt and as a result I was bankrupt. I thought someone was going to come and take absolutely everything off me and it very nearly did happen like that.

Instead we met with a really nice man called Jeremy from Begbies Traynor (liquidation company). Jeremy was a really distinguished man, you could tell he was well educated and had a very polite air about him, whilst putting you at ease with the odd wisecrack as well. He had a glint in his eye like an excitable child in a sweet shop.

Jeremy explained our options to us and agreed that it was a real shame that we hadn't been able to make it work, he could see that the numbers from London were impressive and if even any of the other exhibitions had been half as successful we really had had a good chance. He told us to think carefully about our options, that we could in theory keep trading in the best interest of the company's creditors.

I was worried that I could be in real trouble because the company owed out so much money, not the case according to Jeremy and the advice that we got. Every decision I had made for the company was in both the company's and that of their creditor's best interests. We hired the best sponsorship company and they didn't deliver but even with that we had done due diligence and research to work with 'supposedly' an industry leader. Jeremy could see where the business had failed, and we had all of our emails etc. to back up our story.

Jeremy could see that there was a sound business model and that the company could have a future. If only all the discussions with regards to potential exhibitions for 2019, like the Birmingham NEC etc. had been formally secured, then placing the company into Administration would have been the best way forward. However, without any form of guaranteed income beyond the end of 2018, the only option would be liquidation unless something dramatic happened over the next few weeks.

He could see how upset we were and how much it meant to us and suggested that we give it at least another week in Watford. It was Black Friday weekend at the end of November and the following weekend was the first weekend of December where everyone would get paid and be out Christmas shopping. Surely the shopping centre would get much busier and as such the exhibition would pick up a bit. If this happened, then the tour around other intu shopping centres might just happen meaning there was guaranteed income into 2019 and as such the company could be placed in Administration, restructured and then have a bright future.

We worked out how many people we needed to get per day to sustain the exhibition to ensure there was no wrongful trading and to start paying off some debts. I can't remember now but I am sure it was around 100 people a day to keep us going. The most we reached that weekend was 34 on the Sunday and so by the Sunday evening we knew the exhibition would never open again and the company would have to cease trading with immediate effect and be placed into liquidation.

Deciding to close it and not open again was the hardest decision I have had to make. How could I give up on this dream, the dream to tour the world paying tribute to the biggest girl group ever. Representing the Spice Girls in a positive way, paying tribute with the biggest music exhibition in the world and getting to have fun whilst doing it. It was never about an easy ride, we were always willing to work hard and put the effort in to get the job done. It was a passion project that I believed in 100% and that at certain times has been undoubtedly one of the highlights of my life.

That Sunday night, we pulled the shutters down and played Goodbye by the Spice Girls as we went out live to social media. That was the shock moment, I was behind that camera absolutely breaking my heart and was in a total sense of shock that here I was having to announce to the world the exhibition was closed with immediate effect. I don't think I slept that night. I broke my heart that it was done. There was nothing I could do now. The decision was made. We had given it that last weekend to see if it would pick up at all and it hadn't. If we kept going, I as the Managing Director of the company could get into trouble for wrongful trading, and as such I had to close the exhibition. I knew it wasn't working and there was no way of getting it back and made the decision at 5.55pm on Sunday 25 November 2018 that it was all over.

We were defeated and broken. We always knew that there was a chance we could lose it all. We always knew that we were putting everything we had on the line, including the collection. We just didn't for one second think that with all of the work and years of effort that it would turn out like this.

One of the stupidest things I have ever heard is that

in order to make yourself go bankrupt or place your company into voluntary liquidation you have to pay for it. So, when you have below zero in the bank, you are admitting that either you are personally bankrupt or your company is insolvent and can't pay anything back, but you have to pay to do that and it's not cheap, it's thousands of pounds. What the fuck?

Normally when you appoint a liquidator, they subcontract to another company to come in and access your assets and do the job on the pretence that they will get paid out of the sale of your assets. Then any further money realised from the sale of the assets above the liquidator's fee gets distributed to the company's creditors in a priority order. Well here we were with almost £100K (purchase price) worth of staging, mannequins, shop fittings and everything else you can imagine for the exhibition with a net value of just under £80K and their contractor says it is only worth £2K!

In order to get the company into liquidation, I or the company was going to have to pay the liquidator's £3,000. I don't understand this system at all and was completely taken aback. Nobody to help you when you have gone tits up, unless you pay for it. The only other way of doing it without paying for it, is to wait until some company takes you to court and applies to make you bankrupt, by that point the bailiffs will already have been round and removed everything you own. It doesn't go through the process until all of that happens.

Basically, if you can't pay to put yourself into liquidation or bankruptcy then you have to sit and wait for bailiffs, wait until someone comes and takes away absolutely everything you own and when and only when that has happened will somebody apply to have you made bankrupt. No wonder people kill themselves when they get into financial difficulty.

Whatever we had to do, we were going to do it, we still had to remove all the collections of costumes and memorabilia and get them home, but as for all of the company assets i.e. staging, mannequins etc, that all had to get left for the liquidators to sort out.

I think this was the only silver lining in any of it all. We were physically broken, we had never got ourselves back up on our feet and so at least we now didn't have to move hundreds of mannequins and millions of staging. The collection was hard enough to move on its own but without the staging and everything it was much easier, physically at least. Emotionally, we all cried packing it up, and by us all I mean me and Steven really as nobody else was there to help.

Faye my friend from Cyprus came down to help me on the second day and helped me pack most of the collection items back into boxes and cases.

Everything is a bit of a blur and a bit numb even when I think about it now, I don't really remember pulling it apart or getting it back to the house. Everything was on autopilot at this point. I was literally like a walking zombie. Steven would make sure there was food, make sure that I was drinking water, taking my medications, going to bed. I really was just a shell, walking around trying not to cry or scream and shout.

The phone is still ringing off the hook and we really had been forced to make a decision about the future of the company. Even if the Watford exhibition picked up enough to continue trading, one of our creditors (the PR Company) had obtained a county court judgement against the company and had immediately applied to the high court for an enforcement order. As much as I might take issue with some of the other creditors of the company in this book, I have to say that they all understood the position and realised the best way to try and recoup any of the money they were owed was to give the company time to try and trade it out in Watford and secure the company's future into 2019 and beyond. Even the Business Design Centre made an offer to delay action, but their terms were not acceptable. The only creditor to take this course of action and immediately enforce it was the PR Company and that was ultimately the final nail in Spice Girls' Exhibition Ltd.'s coffin.

The major problem with the High Court Enforcement Order obtained by the PR company is they had obtained it against our home address, completely illegal and unlawful and they only ever had our home address because they used my address for the car that was taking us to ITV. Other than that, they had never had any need to have my home address and the company address which is where the enforcement order should have been made against was completely different.

Nevertheless, they managed to get the CCJ and a High Court Enforcement Order which now meant that they could at any time send in the bailiffs to collect on the debt. Of course we told them and the debt company and the court that they had the wrong address, but nobody would listen.

Every day I was a nervous wreck thinking that someone was coming into our house and taking my collection away from me in bin bags. Worse than that I still had other people's collections in my house and I was worried about them. There was no legal way they could take them as they did not belong to the company plus, we had the contract of loan from the other collectors and designers.

Putting the company into liquidation isn't an immediate thing and there is lots of stuff you have to do to even get the process going. I say stuff because, Steven handles most of the legalities of the company on my behalf. I am really hopeless at paperwork, forms scare me, and I get really frustrated with them. Without Steven, none of this would have got done, and I would have been the guy sitting in the corner of the room with nothing round about me after the bailiffs had left.

The phone is still ringing constantly, the exhibition is closed, and we are also having to deal with the fall out of that. People want to know what went wrong, some people (not many granted) had booked tickets in advance and were contacting us about that of course. Fans quite rightly feel ownership of it and quite rightly were asking questions all over social media.

Two days had passed since we closed and still no bailiffs, so at least that was a positive thing.

I had already started selling off parts of the collection by this point, selling it through a friend's eBay so that nobody would pick up on the fact that it was me selling. Some of this money was starting to help pay for the liquidation but we had to borrow even more money from my father-in-law at this point. If we hadn't or he hadn't been able to lend us any, we would have been homeless by Christmas for sure.

Three days after we had closed and still no bailiffs......

We were chasing as much as we could to try and get everything together, there was a lot of paperwork involved and we had to get everything that we could about the company together and ready to hand over to the liquidators.

Neither of us were sleeping at all, worried sick about someone coming through the door, about all the threats of court action we were getting. We had personally guaranteed a few of the company loans so now every penny, even in our personal banks was getting taken away as fast as it was going in.

Four days after we had closed and still no bailiffs…..

Reversing out the driveway to take Steven to his work and go to the post office to post a few of the items I had sold on eBay and halfway out the driveway, a van pulls across the driveway behind me.

"There's the bailiffs Steven."

I knew straight away what it was and who they were, I could tell and instantly my stomach flipped, and I felt sick.

First rule with a bailiff is don't let them in but not Steven. Steven is sure he has it all covered with contracts and has all the legalities covered:

"Come on in guys."

What a fucking nightmare Steven is sometimes, of course the bailiffs came in the house and were not interested in listening to anything we said. They knew the costumes were there, they knew exactly what they were looking for and even mentioned a few costumes by design without seeing them.

Steven showed them all of the legal contracts we had proving that a lot of them were on loan and didn't belong to the company. They couldn't care less and said the owners would have to go to court to prove ownership. They were taking them away unless we paid the debt in full.

This was full blown panic stations for me, I had listened to Jeremy and I had listened to Steven who both told me this would not be the situation, yet here I am with two bailiffs in my house manhandling some of the most iconic Spice Girls' costumes ever.

The first thing we did was phone the liquidators and see if there was anything they could do, they spoke to the company's legal team and told them they had no right to be at our home address etc. but they were not for budging. Instead they ordered a van to come to the house and made me start listing the items.

Steven kept working with the liquidators whilst I continued to list costume pieces one by one taking as much time as I could. We tried to keep it friendly with the two guys, but they were usual bailiffs and were not interested, instead remaining stand-offish.

What became clear is that the bailiffs could not remove one single item from the house without first having it inventoried and that the full contents had to go at one time. They couldn't take some of it and come back for the rest.

It was at this point I said to them

> "Right guys well you better pitch down for the long haul, there are over 7,000 items of Spice Girls' memorabilia in this house and it is literally going to take us three or four days to inventory it."

Steven and I could both see the realisation come over

both of their faces, we had now been sitting writing down a list of costumes for half an hour, and with the level of description required I was on costume 8 or 9.

It became a little bit of a stretch it out exercise for us as we were sitting hoping against all hope that there would be something that the liquidators could do for us.

The bailiffs were on the phone constantly, chasing the removals van, speaking to their boss and taking direction from the office. They were standing firm and the realisation that they might actual take all of this Spice Girls' memorabilia was actually becoming a bit too much of a real-life nightmare. With every second that passed it seemed less and less likely that we were going to be able to sort the situation and that they might actually drive away with all of these costumes in the back of a bloody van.

Then as I was sitting listing the costumes for the bailiffs to take away, Steven got a call from our liquidators and at that moment it looked like someone was looking over us.

Having a Scottish registered company had been an absolute pain in the ass at times. It had stopped us from getting loads of things in place and always made the finance process of any kind much more complicated.

Steven put the phone down, and I could see that he was full of business, he stood up walked to the kitchen and then shouted on me.

"Come here a minute Alan."

As I walked to the kitchen, I hoped beyond all hope that something was going to be able to be done. We simply didn't have the money to pay this debt and not only that we would have disputed the amount by a significant difference. We owed the PR company £12K, yet they had gone to court to pursue us for a claim of £19K. I know we were in a tough position and we didn't dispute that the company owed them the money, but they were absolutely taking the piss just adding an additional £7K and then getting a court to action it.

> "Alan, because the company is a Scottish registered company, we can put it into administration instantly, normally if it is an English registered company the process takes a minimum of 48 hours but because it is Scottish law, Begbies Traynor Scottish office can have it placed into administration now. We have a couple of forms to fill in which they are going to send us through now."

Please don't get me wrong, we were not disputing that the company owed people money, we were sick to death worried about it and had been for months but this, this was wrong on so many levels and the PR company had done everything they possibly could to target the costumes. The costumes were never owned by the company, especially not other people's costumes, so what they were trying to do was underhanded and dickish, for want of a better word. We had informed them of the address mistake, they ignored it and got the court to enforce. Lying to a court is completely illegal and this company gave the instruction to go ahead despite knowing full well what they were doing was wrong, not only that they had also been dickish in adding on an additional £7K. I felt bad, it's awful when someone owes you money and we were now down and out.

I will always have to live with the fact that some people will not get paid the money that they are owed from the company because the assets in the company were not enough to pay everything off. I will forever be sorry to these people. People like the Guestlist London or Simply Business Moves, who absolutely worked their assess off for us. Also, individual people who work for larger companies like Richard and his team at the Hilton. Guys I am truly sorry my company failed. I never set out for it to end up this way.

But, and this is a small but, and also only a small part of me, but to the Business Design Centre who had kept us hostage, to the PR company who broke every legal rule in trying to enforce the debt and then add £7K on top, at this moment in time, at this exact moment where I was sitting listing my own personal collection of iconic costumes along with other people's, in order for bailiffs to take them away. At this exact moment I wouldn't have pissed on these people if they were on fire.

The PR company, I understand their frustration, I don't understand their tactics, but I do understand they worked hard.

With the Business Design Centre, even sitting there a broken man, I would never ever give into them, and never will. Max and the Business Design Centre, I stand by my original statement and always will 'Apologise to my PA Alex and buy her some flowers to say sorry'. I have said this from day one, until you do the gentlemanly thing, I will never speak to you as a gentleman. You allowed the situation to get out of hand, do the decent thing.

Jackie Fast, yeah, fast one.

Anyway, as you can tell from the above this still upsets me.

Steven was busy printing off pages and pages of paperwork whilst I continued to list the bloody costumes. We were now hoping we could get the company into liquidation before the bailiffs could start taking any of the costumes belonging to anyone else away.

"Sign this, sign this and sign this."

There was then a lot of scanning of documents and frantic sending of emails back and forward to the liquidation company, the whole time I am having to sit there and go through these costumes that meant the world to me for someone else to take away and the bigger bailiff (to be honest they were both huge guys) hangs up the phone call he was on.

"Thanks very much for your co-operation today, we will be leaving now."

The bailiffs both shook our hands and said that normally these things were a nightmare for them. Through the whole process we had tried to stay calm, be nice to them, invite them in and offer them cups of tea. They were only doing their job, however uncomfortable it was for us.

As the door closed behind them, I couldn't even stand up. I sat on the couch, shuddering and crying. It was the strangest moment of my entire life.

On one hand I was beyond devastated that my company was actually and officially now folded and that I would never be able to have another Spice Girls' Exhibition again. On the other hand, it had come so close to two guys actually carrying every item of my collection, but worse other people's collections out of my house, and it would have been the worst kind of nightmare trying to get anything back from them.

I was broke, relieved, disappointed and completely numb. How the fuck did we get here! This amazing exhibition that we have created. The biggest music exhibition there has ever been, in the UK at least, but most probably the world with over 300 costume pieces on show. How did it end up with bailiffs at my house, holding Geri Halliwell's Olympics costume amongst others?

I was sick to my stomach, I don't think I ate for days, and at this point everything really becomes a blur for weeks and weeks.

It was over, there was nothing we could do now to save it, all those months and months and months of working night and day, spending every single day at the exhibition for months on end, running guided tours, smiling at the front desk and chatting excitedly with every visitor.

It was all done. All gone.

My memory of the weeks that followed is really bad, I know it was the middle of December and I knew we had to move house two days before Christmas, we couldn't continue to live in our current house as it was now too expensive and we were falling behind on the rent, so had no choice but to downsize.

I slept for days on end, not washing, not changing out of my pyjamas, not eating or eating junk food. I just seemed to spiral into a hopeless dark hole where nothing was worth anything and nothing mattered. There was a difference this time. It wasn't a hole of self-destructive blackness, like I have had previously, that have led to previous suicide attempts. It was a hole like a cocoon, almost like a reflective chamber. Whatever was going on I needed time to process it and be numb, to sit and think in my own head if there was anything we could have done differently but not only that just to process everything that has happened in 2018. It had been a rollercoaster year from start to finish, a year that has completely changed my life forever, that has changed me as a person.

I'll never be the same person I was before the exhibition, before losing Nand or before having my thyroid out. That person was suicidal and had no belief or self-worth. Whatever the journey will teach me in the long run I've learned that life is way too short. I am glad we took the chance to follow my dream and give it everything we could. I am truly gutted that the company folded owing so much money to other companies, that was never our intention and I do have to live with that but it's not worth my life and I hope even our biggest creditor would agree that.

I've changed. I don't know if it is the impact of having my thyroid removed. I'm not as depressed or naturally anxious as I was before my operation but maybe it was Nand that changed me? Maybe losing someone so close gives you the kick up the bum you need to just get bloody on with it. Not only that but to give it the best shot you can with everything! Maybe it was the togetherness of the team and the support network I had and have around me?

I don't know what it is, but what I do know is that I will always be devastated that the company didn't work. I am devastated that I have to sell off my beloved collection to pay off loans I have personally guaranteed. Shit happens. However, I will never ever put a noose around my neck again. I will never ever allow myself to be in that place again. So, maybe it's a costly one, but it's definitely a lesson learned.

The other lesson I have learned, is that the Spice Girls inspired me. They virtually held my hand as I was growing up and told me to believe in myself. I didn't know them personally, but like so many millions of fans around the world, they reached out that hand of friendship when I was vulnerable and told me to dream big, work hard and try hard, but above all do everything with passion and believe in yourself.

I don't need to own costumes they wore on tour or award discs that they won. I don't need the buffalo shoes, the thousands of items of merchandise or hundreds of dolls to feel closer to the Spice Girls. They influenced my attitude to myself and that I will always have with me.

People keep messaging me absolutely gorgeous messages of support, especially when they see items up for sale but hey, nobody died, life goes on thankfully.

I don't know what is next for me, the next couple of months I am getting to follow the girls around on their reunion tour, something that has always been a lifelong dream for me. I'm going to all 13 of their UK concerts and have loads of fun lined up around it.

It feels like a nice way to sign off, telling the truth with this book, apologising to fans, and everyone that feels let down, trying to draw a line and move on with our lives.

One thing is for sure. No more exhibitions but a lot more downtime with my husband. The man is my guardian angel and I have neglected him enough. I can't wait to make our relationship the priority in my life, smile more and worry a lot less than I did in the past few years.

Thank you each and every one of you for your incredible support over the past four years, being a part of the Spiceworld family of fans has been an absolute privilege for me and I hope I managed to do our girls justice.

Mr Alan Spice x

25

Knowing the Girls are Happy

One thing I felt I had to do when the exhibition ended was, out of courtesy, let the girls and their management know what the situation was. We had so much press coverage around the world I was now worried that it was going to be picked up and cause a kind of negative backlash or press for the girls themselves.

I messaged the mums and let them know what was happening, emailed their lawyer and sent a message to Melanie C. It wasn't anything major just along the lines of… "The company has gone into liquidation and unfortunately we have had to close the doors on our beloved exhibition for the last time. We are worried that this may have any negative press attention and wanted to as a courtesy inform you of the situation ourselves."

The messages were sent out around 2pm and by 6pm that same day I had an email from the amazing Melanie C's manager.

I would never share the full email, but it was along the lines of, "We are so sorry to hear about the exhibition especially when we know you have worked so hard on it. Melanie is concerned about you and asked me to email you straight away to see if there is anything we can do to help you personally."

They didn't need to email me back and I have always been of the opinion that the girls owe me absolutely nothing. It wasn't for recognition or any other motive, I simply wanted to be able to showcase my collection in the best way I could, if I could make a living from it even better, but that wasn't to be.

Here I am, a real Spice Girl has emailed me to make sure I am okay, not overly worried about anything else, but first and foremost worried about me and my health.

There were a few conversations back and forth after that with the Spice Girls' management team and a few other people involved in their business side. With the tour happening in 2019 it was such a shame that the exhibition wouldn't continue.

Despite the conversations back and forth we have never been able to make anything work between us. I think the Spice Girls are such a huge machine that not one person can ever make a definitive decision. It's a bit like the intu situation where everyone has to sign everything off and then it goes to the next person.

We still had and still have debts that we have to pay off and in order to do that I have to sell my beloved collection off. There was never any talk of the girls gifting anything financially but there was maybe a mention of buying or renting the collection in order to help me out of the personal situation I was in.

The fact that this ever came up in the conversation was a massive boost for me personally. I hadn't pissed them off, in fact, they were trying everything they could to now help me out.

I had a telephone conversation with Melanie C's manager Joe one day and I explained this to him. The only thing I was worried about was letting the girls down in any way. Joe was so kind in assuring me that the girls knew all about the exhibition and that they had been delighted by the response to it.

It was really hard for me to keep it together on the phone at this point, and like a huge loser I began to get really emotional with Joe. I could hear Melanie talking in the background and asking him questions and I was gone. Joe could obviously tell that I was getting a bit upset as he was becoming a bit worried. He told me to go get myself a drink and calm myself down and we would talk soon.

We did talk again a couple of times and I was passed over to the Spice Girls' management at Modest eventually. However, the situation is so complicated both at our side and at theirs, that ultimately, I think there are just too many hurdles to overcome to make anything happen.

Another amazing thing that happened was a message from Pauline Bunton. This happened just before we were leaving Manchester and Pauline offered to give me Emma's Spiceworld tour case. It is a huge rolling tour case that you could fit five people into. It has Spiceworld stamped on the side of it and Emma was kind enough to sign it for me.

I was stuck at the exhibition every day, so Steven had to hire a van and go to Pauline's house to pick it up. I was beyond devastated that I couldn't go and say hi in person, but it needed to be picked up and so off Steven went. Jade, Emma's partner who is also a singer from 'Damage' came out of the house to meet Steven and he said he chatted away for ages, talking about the exhibitions and saying sorry they missed it.

Steven is not up on any form of celebrity and had absolutely no idea who Jade was, "I think it was Emma's husband maybe, a good looking black bald guy?" OMG Steven you dick that is Jade, and you better not have said anything stupid to him haha. I don't give my husband credit, Jade was probably quite happy that Steven wasn't some huge crazy fan.

Knowing that the girls knew about the exhibition, that the mums had been to see it in Manchester and enjoyed the trip down memory lane, but also in London Victoria Beckham's mum and dad had been and of course Natalie Halliwell Jennings. I still keep in touch with Natalie occasionally on social media. She is incredibly warm and friendly and I feel so lucky to now count her as a friend. There is a warning on that though Natalie, once I am a friend, I am a friend for life and that's just the way it is.

At the end of it, the girls are happy and we managed to do them justice. The biggest girl band ever deserved the biggest music exhibition ever. Along with thanks to the other collectors from around the world, I was able to create the biggest, most appropriate tribute I could to five living legends that changed the course of my life.

In some ways, it's job done, as the Spice Girls said in 2007 'Mission Accomplished'. It's not quite how I wanted it to end or turn out, we should be in New York or somewhere else exciting with it, welcoming guests and taking them around the costumes and memorabilia, but that's not to be.

I wish the girls could have seen it in person as it will never be replicated on that scale ever again, we did get apologies from a couple for that, but we always understood they were busy, that their schedules are booked months in advance and to top it all off we had organised it at the height of summer. When the exhibition opened in London, four out of the five Spice Girls were on Holiday.

It's not the ending we were hoping for, but it was one hell of a ride, and I think I managed to pay a suitable tribute to these five ladies that changed lives all around the globe.

Spice Girls Forever!

26

Wait, What About the Bomb on the Bus?

The Spice Bus!

The Bloody Spice Bus!

Don't talk to me about the bloody Spice Bus!

There was one piece of advice that I had been given from Nand that if I could go back and change anything I would listen to that advice.

> "Concentrate on your bread and butter, what you're good at, forget about all the added extras, they will only bring additional hassle."

As usual, Nand was spot on.

Whilst it was a privilege to be involved with the bus and I was totally in awe of it the first time that I saw it, I really should have left it alone. It was too big a project for me on top of everything else and it was and still is a huge money pit.

The bus has been left to rot for almost twenty years since the movie. At one point the Spice Girls' fan club bought it and tried to save it from the scrapyard, but the storage costs were becoming too much and so it had to be sold on.

It was bought by a man called Eamon who owns the Isle of Wight Marina and he was clever enough to buy it as a tourist attraction for the harbour. In the grand scheme of things, Eamon bought the bus for pennies, I can't remember the exact figure, but it was definitely not more than a couple of thousand pounds.

He moved it over to the Isle of Wight and had even gone as far as to have some plans drawn up to have the bus converted into some kind of holiday accommodation. I've seen the plans and they are actually pretty stunning but lacked any kind of Spice Girls' touch. There was no reference to the original design or even any kind of major reflection of the girls at all inside.

With the size of the outside space at the venue in London I had the crazy idea of having the Spice Bus as part of the exhibition. Had I left it as an idea it wouldn't have caused so many headaches but then again if I had left it as an idea, I am unsure that the bus would be preserved at all. At least now I know it has a good future ahead of it.

I'd initially contacted the marina to see about the possibility of borrowing the bus and was put on to an amazingly interesting man called Darren. Darren and I chatted about what I wanted to do, our original chat was way back when I lived in Cyprus. It seemed to take forever to get anything agreed even in principle, but we got there.

By the time I had moved back to the UK, I was already planning a trip to the Isle of Wight to see the bus and see what needed to be done for myself.

I knew that there was a lot of passion for the Spice Bus, it had been so heavily involved in the Spice World movie and fans were constantly talking about it online.

After having a chat with Andy from gassProductions we realised quickly the interest in the bus and also that we could create a lot of interest for the exhibition with footage of the bus.

There was one problem, the bus was a total wreck! It needed new tyres, it would start sometimes and then cut out, the gears were not working, there were air leaks everywhere (I nodded and pretended to know what that meant), and the inside of it was like a skip.

We went to the Isle of Wight to do some filming with it and to be honest this was great fun. Andy and I on a little Spice Girls filming adventure creating a buzz for social media was a lot of fun. Andy is charming company and we had a lot of laughs on our little road trip.

It's also where one of the most magical moments of the exhibition happened. Andy and I had been filming in London with the designers, filming at the venue and then filming with the designers before we headed to the Isle of Wight. It had been a long few days, but the interest online was really getting huge.

The day we got to the harbour and we were going to see the bus (which was parked at a farm down the road) we got a phone call from the farm manager to let us know that there were a couple of photographers and press up at the bus waiting for us to arrive. It seems that the social media coverage was working and any PR was good PR at this point.

This was the most surreal moment ever, driving up a country lane, going to see this iconic Spice Girls' Bus, Andy and I were like giddy school kids. Andy was telling me the plan of action when we got there. He wanted to capture my reaction at seeing the bus for the first time but also interacting with the press.

This was totally bonkers!

We were out in the middle of nowhere and waiting for us were a couple of people with cameras from local newspapers and of course Andy with his filming rig, filming everything that was going on.

The moment I saw the bus, the moment I saw the huge Union Jack on wheels, my stomach was churning with butterflies. Not nerves, nothing but sheer delight. She was so incredibly beautiful and imposing that it really did take me a moment to take in what we were doing.

I have absolutely no idea what I said to anyone I just know that I was in awe of this magnificent, vibrant, mega piece of Spice Girls' history.

The bus is huge, it's not quite the size that they make out in the movie and of course the inside was just an old derelict bus, but nevertheless it is a huge vintage double decker bus and makes quite an impression with her Union Jack coat on.

Not only did we get to see the bus, but the owners agreed to let us ride on it down to the harbour where we were going to be doing some filming of her for a fundraising campaign.

I'd realised that the only way we were going to make the bus project work was with a crowdfunding campaign. A way for the Spice fans to get involved and help to save the bus from the scrapyard. The issue was, nobody could have predicted the actual cost of having the bus renovated to a state where it was even driveable.

The plan was to have it renovated inside so that it resembled the scene of the movie as far as was possible. It was never going to be exact. The inside of the Spice Bus was like the inside of the Tardis, it didn't actually exist and was all filmed in a studio.

We did have plans to fit in aspects of it and make it as authentic an experience as possible. There would be the outline of Baby Spice's playhouse, there was a cross trainer for Sporty and a catwalk for Posh, but that's as far as it got really.

I had no idea how to fix a bus so we went about researching companies that could do it and that had experience with other older buses. In fact, the company we used were recommended to us, although we were warned they were pricey.

SEC or South East Coachworks were who we had begun to work with and we had a meeting with them eventually at their offices in Kent.

The problems began when they carried out work to the bus that we hadn't signed off and that we had no idea needed doing. We were on a limited budget; we had managed to raise around £7,000 from a Spice Girls' fans Crowdfunder and anything beyond that would need to be covered by the company or by other deals to rent the bus out for events.

What we needed was the inside of the bus up to some kind of standard that resembled the movie. We also needed the bus to look like it did in the movie from the outside and I am sure we could have covered all of this no problem.

What happened was, supposedly the bus turned up to the bus depot and the floor fell out of it, so before anything else they had to install a whole new floor on the bottom level at a cost of £20,000. Then also supposedly the bus needed £12,500 worth of mechanical work before it would be able to drive to any venue.

The worst part was, 'supposedly' the work had already been carried out on the bus as there was no reasonable alternative.

How is it reasonable to carry out over £30,000 of

work on a bus before getting the go ahead?

Honestly if I had known the extent at this stage and that they were just going to do any work they saw fit, in any order without even checking, I would have sent the bus back to the Isle of Wight.

It wasn't my bus. I was trying to make it a part of our exhibition whilst saving this iconic piece of pop music history. The only problem is, the crowdfunding was not anywhere near that level and soon all the promises of working partnerships that we had been promised from SEC were nowhere to be seen.

They had been talking about a bakeries tour with one of their other clients to try and recoup costs, but did nothing to make it work.

They wanted to capitalise on the marketing value of working on the bus but were unwilling to offset any of that value against the costs.

They went ahead and did any work they wanted rather than the actual work we needed done to make it exhibition ready.

They were demanding tens of thousands of pounds for work that was supposedly already carried out on the bus, and then despite paying for the mechanics they also wanted to charge us for all the breakdown fees when she broke down straight away after £12K of mechanical work.

One of the invoices SEC sent us for mechanical works

on the bus was an invoice for £900 to have the windscreen wipers replaced. New window wiper motors, new window wipers and labour. Nearly a thousand pounds for windscreen wipers, are you having a laugh? Not only that but by the time the bus got to London it had to stop because there was a rain shower and the windscreen wipers were not working. Hmmm.

The bus was amazing, it was wonderful and having it as part of the London exhibition really felt like a massive Union Jack landmark for the whole thing. It was also really popular, people loved it and it pulled in the crowds.

Standing outside the London venue watching her drive up into the car park and take pride of place as a beacon of Girl Power was one of the best moments ever. It was causing us all sorts of headaches but here she was in all of her splendid red, white and blue glory.

The next headache to deal with was the plaques that so many people had donated a lot of money to have on the bus. SEC had assured us this was another part of their business and they would easily be able to install the plaque wall for us.

Despite sending over all the details for the plaques, of course they didn't do it. It wasn't £1,000 for windscreen wipers so they just simply didn't bother their arse and also didn't bother telling us until the day before. So here we are in full blown exhibition set up mode and we now have to arrange for plaques for the bus. People had pledged a lot of money and there was no option of not having them.

It cost us almost £500 to have the plaques made last minute and they were nothing like what we wanted for them. The most important thing at this point was to get the plaques on the bus for fans to see when they were visiting.

Disaster struck when the plaques couldn't be made for another few days and then when we eventually did get them on the bus some bastard came along and stole them.

First it was Rylan's plaque that was taken, who had pledged hundreds of pounds to help the bus project, then it was another and another and another. Why would you steal a dedication plaque with someone else's name on it? I don't get the sense in this at all.

With that aside this was the only thing that really went wrong with the bus in London.

SEC were taking the bus after London for a couple of days to do some more work on it and then they were bringing it up to Manchester for the Manchester launch evening.

Now please bear in mind we have been told that there has been over £12K of mechanics done on the bus to make her roadworthy and reliable. Since then she has driven from Kent to central London and back to Kent. The next time she was to be moved was on her way to Manchester and guess what.

She broke down.

Not only did she break down, but she broke down on the motorway and press managed to get pictures of it at the side of the road. To add icing on top SEC were now refusing to deliver the bus to Manchester unless we paid them the £2,000 recovery costs from the motorway.

These guys were taking the piss, not only that but they knew this was going to have a massive impact on the exhibition. A whole part of the arrival in Manchester and creating a PR buzz, given there was no money for PR or marketing for Manchester, had been having the bus driving around the city with Spice Girls' music blaring out. Now instead of a Union Jack fanfare we had to try and explain to thousands of visitors why the bus was not there.

The bus was now being held to ransom with us, the guys knew how popular it was with our visitors so used that to demand recovery costs that I would never have paid any other time. Recovery costs as well as a ridiculous mechanical bill, you're having a laugh. Nevertheless, the only way we were getting the bus was shelling out more money to these guys, so we scraped it together and eventually got the bus up to Manchester for the second Manchester exhibition at the Great Northern Warehouse.

I don't know why we bothered, remember from earlier in the book, we averaged about 20 to 30 people a day at the second venue in Manchester. The damage was done, if the bus had been there from the start it might have been a different story, but we never really gathered momentum and I am sure that was a part of it.

The bus also became a huge target in the middle of Manchester. It wasn't like in London where it was off the main street and was quite secure. It was now parked right in the middle of Manchester city centre and that attracted all sorts of issues.

It had never been locked once in London and we had absolutely no hassles with it at all, it had been left open all night every night and nobody went near it.

Manchester was a different story and it took us all our efforts to make sure that someone didn't simply drive off in it. Northerners are a lot bolder than southerners, so it was straight in the driver seat, straight away looking for the ignition or the hand break or the gears.

With it being on a slope I was constantly worrying about it taking off and rolling down through one of Manchester's busiest roads. People were being reckless with it. Not only that but one morning we found some drunk guy sleeping on the bus! Apparently, he didn't make it home from a night out so decided to sleep it off on the bus! In the end it sat in Manchester locked up most of the time.

We didn't have the staff numbers to supervise it all of the time and it wasn't fair to ask anyone to go outside and watch the bus in the pouring rain or freezing cold in case some idiot couldn't understand a 'do not touch' sign.

The bus was one of the last major dramas for us in Manchester. Again, if we look back in the book, we mentioned just how broke we were when we were leaving Manchester.

The relationship with SEC had completely broken down and they completely refused to move the bus unless we paid them an amount of money. I can't remember how much, maybe £3 or £5K, but it didn't matter how much, we didn't have it and there was no way we could get it.

The only thing I could do with the bus at this point was phone the owner and tell him the situation. We had a contract with him that they would not be put to cost other than that disclosed, and that it was our responsibility to return the bus to them.

I had to phone Eamon and tell him there was no way I was able to move the bus, no way I could get the money together and if I couldn't get help from somewhere I would have to go to the police station and tell them the bus was abandoned in the square.

The police would have impounded the bus and the press nightmare that would have caused would have finished us off for sure.

Thankfully, Eamon was a gentleman and agreed to recover the bus to his yard at his own cost.

We were full of hopes and aspirations for the bus but ultimately, I should have listened to my little friend Nand and concentrated on the main event.

So, what happened to the bomb on the bus? I actually have no idea, but I do know that there are times where I could quite happily have put a bomb on her myself.

What I do know is that she now has a very bright future and thanks to those crowdfunding donations and having the bus involved with the exhibition, we ignited the passion for her again. I'd say watch this space, but I know that by the time the book is out there should be major news of her next adventure.

I'm looking forward to seeing her again.

27

The Missing Chapter – A Gift

The gift is the best I have ever been given.

I have received many amazing gifts. My engagement and wedding rings. Emma Bunton's massive Spiceworld trunk that she hand signed is without doubt the most significant piece in my collection and within the exhibition – the very first sign of approval from the one and only Baby Spice.

But those are nowhere near the best gift I have ever been given, as ultimately they are material items.

The gift I am talking about here came from Nand and Stevie C. The gift of pushing me to believe in myself but also educating me on how to just let things go. Something I have never been very good at.

Let it go, sometimes there are things in life that you can't control, like a doctor lying, or something else as equally unjust but completely out of your control.

Nand and Stevie C together showed me that I was spending so much energy and time being upset about things that it was having an effect on everything else in my life. Yes, the situation I was in was shit and unjust but here I was spending months of my life being beyond raging about it, beyond upset with it upsetting me, making me physically and mentally ill and I couldn't let it go.

They made it make sense somehow and reinforced what each other was saying to me at different times. Watching 'The Secret' with Stevie C in Cyprus is single-handedly the most enlightening moment I have ever had in my life.

Then there was all the time I was spending with Nand. We could get in a car have a rant, get it out of our systems with each other and practise letting it go, moving on from it, taking a deep breath and shaking it off.

As your blood is beginning to boil or you about to lose the plot with someone, take a step back, look at the situation and see if there is realistically anything you can do to change it in a positive way, if not, drop it, let it go.

It's all about how you channel your energy. If you spend all of your energy being angry and upset then that is generally what you get back in life whereas if you can take a deep breath let it go, then you can turn that energy that you would have spent on being angry or upset, on something positive, into making something else work.

This is a gift. This is the gift. This is the thing that changed my life. It changed my whole attitude towards myself and my daily routine and really helped me to get my head down and crack on with getting things done.

This is the missing chapter of the book, the bit of the book that I have had to shy away from writing, that I had to wait until the end to write.

Nand and Stevie C changed my life and gave me the tools to look at the positive rather than focussing on the negative, and without that I wouldn't have got through the past year. I wouldn't have got out of Cyprus alive and it makes me sad every day that Nand will never know just how much she changed my life.

It's hard to write about loss, it's hard to write about losing your best friend just when you needed her the most. It's a real mixture of emotions.

Nand had been fighting a great battle against cancer, the first time round she kicked its arse with surgery and cannabis oil, no shitting you. She couldn't stand the thought of chemo or radiotherapy so went down the alternative route and it worked very well for her, clearing all signs of cancer from her body.

Sometime later (maybe 18 months) something had been niggling and she had a pain in her shoulder when we were in Cyprus. Nand had asked me to rub deep heat on to it as she thought it was maybe a muscle she had pulled at Pilates. It wasn't like Nand to moan about anything and when the pain kept up, she of course went back to the doctor.

Nand would spend half her time in Cyprus and half

her time in her Coventry house near her family. It was perfect for us. In Cyprus we were ten minutes away from each other and now as we were moving back to the UK Nand would still only be a drive away from us.

What we didn't know is that by the time we got back from Cyprus in November, Nand was already a lot sicker and it wasn't long until we had the devastating news that the cancer was back. This time it was in her lungs and her thyroid, and if I remember rightly a couple of other places elsewhere.

I'd go and stay with Nand once a week mostly on a Thursday night into a Friday. We would talk about everything to do with the exhibition. She was my confidante, I trusted everything that she told me, and I always knew there was no other agenda other than wanting to help.

One thing that Nand and I had was a very tactile loving friendship, we always did from the moment we met each other, there was always gentle touching, hands on shoulders, hands over hands, a stroke of the face to say hello.

We constantly split our sides laughing and joking about something completely ridiculous that nobody else would even understand or find the slightest bit funny. There was a natural ability just to make each other laugh and smile without too much effort.

Even if one of us was being grumpy the other knew exactly what to do to break the ice and lighten the mood, pulling a face, farting, showing chewed food or a stupid quote from something or a ridiculous mimic.

We constantly told each other how much we loved each other and what we meant to each other. It was a strange friendship as if we should have been friends our whole lives, as if we had grown up together and could tell each other absolutely anything, and we did. There was no subject we couldn't discuss.

What is hilarious though is that Nand always thought she was good at hiding her feelings or thoughts if she didn't quite like something but her facial expressions gave it away instantly. If she was annoyed there was no way you were mistaking it, but she wouldn't stay annoyed for long, well at least not with me anyway. I'm sure Grandad (Stevie C) would tell you a few stories of her being raging but again what's the point unless it's to laugh about it? What's the point on focussing on that time you fell out about this or that?

Nand was one of the kindest people that I have ever known in my life. I don't like to talk about people's money and neither would Nand, but Nand was comfortable in life and she knew that she was fortunate about that, she used it for good though and without a big fuss would send out boxes of advent calendars to her son Max and all of his army friends for Christmas. Seriously, like 40 selection boxes just so they would all have a present from mummy Nand.

Mummy Nand is funny, I would
referred to Nand as that, she was my n.
she did meet my mum in Glasgow my mun.

> "It's nice to finally meet his Cy⊦
> mummy."

Nand was horrified by this and as soon as we got
back to the hotel room it was:

> "That is not how you think of me is it, your
> Cyprus Mum?"

Hahaha! No, you daft mare you are 'me mate' my
silly muck around, let's get wrecked and have a
laugh mate. Nand's face was a picture.

Nand died on the 27th February 2018 only four
months after we moved back from Cyprus. The
cancer was too much for her and before we knew it,
it had taken over her body and there was nothing
that could be done.

We had spent weeks reminiscing about good times
and trying to keep everything as positive as you
possibly can for someone who knows that the end is
coming. Every time I drove away from Nand's house
in Coventry I had to stop around the corner. I would
howl in my car on my own, sobbing and snotting
everywhere. My heart was breaking and every time I
left Nand's house I was terrified that it was going to
be the last time that I would see my little pink friend.

Then the day came when It happened. The last time I
had left the house in Coventry I had forgotten

nething and had to turn around and go back in. Vhen I got there Nand was in the middle of telling the Marie Curie nurses who I was.

> "What did you forget, I was just telling the ladies how gorgeous you are."

> "Don't worry gorgeous that's me off now, I love you, see you soon."

I never got to see Nand alive again.

Grandad (Stevie C) messaged me on the morning of the 27th to tell me that Nand had to go into hospital because she was feeling really poorly. Sitting there waiting for news was torture and when my phone bleeped with a message to let me know she had passed, my heart broke in two.

I don't actually remember much else, I remember being on the floor in my living room curled up in a ball, hiding my face from the dogs who were obviously instantly worried and trying to lick my face.

Everything about Nand was amazing and inspirational to me, she was a trendsetter of her time and in the seven years that we were friends she always was. People looked up to her, looked to her for inspiration and for help and advice. Nand was a really wise soul in a tiny little pink fluffy body of kindness.

I don't think there was a single bad bone in her body, I do sometimes wish she could handle her drink more as I was constantly having to carry her somewhere at the end of a night out haha.

One thing that Nand was, was a hilarious drunk, she would become even more smiley and expressive than normal but not only that she would instantly be legless, there was no middle ground. She was having fun, the life and soul of the party with pink sparkly hair, pink lippy and sometimes even a pink tutu, but one sip too much of wine and she turned into Mrs Jelly in an instant.

The reason for this chapter, the reason for me to share so much information and all the stories about Nand is not for the sympathy, it's not to say oh poor me look what happened, no it's to highlight just how much this lady, rather like the Spice Girls, changed my life.

Unfortunately, Nand never made it to the launch evening of the exhibition she died exactly five months to the day before it. But we did take Nand to the exhibition with us and in fact, it became tradition that Nand was always the first thing in the exhibition and the last thing out of it.

Nand was Mrs Pink and as I said she had a huge collection of elephant figurines, pictures, lamps and anything else elephant or pink that you can imagine.

The only way we could ever pay tribute to her was with a huge big pink elephant. I knew it was what I wanted to do and I knew we would try and help a cancer charity when doing it but what it turned out was a perfect little tribute to my little bestie.

If you came to the exhibition, whether it was in London, Manchester or Watford, one of the first things you would have seen as you walked in the door would have been a life-sized baby pink elephant all covered in sparkles. It was our metaphorical 'Elephant in the room' as well as paying an amazing tribute to my little Nand we teamed up with Breast Cancer Care and helped to raise a little bit of money and awareness for the charity.

The other good thing about it was Nand hadn't gone anywhere, every single time I walked into the exhibition I could see her there in the shape of a pink elephant. It made me smile every single day without fail. I'd never chat to it or anything creepy like that, but it felt like Nand was there, watching over us and keeping me safe.

You could have got us more sponsorships ya bitch haha only kidding my gorgeous friend.

My take on losing Nand is quite simple:

> "It's hard to be sad about losing someone when you are just so bloody grateful to have had them in your life at all."

Every time I see something pink or something glittery or an elephant, I think of my little pink bestie and smile, remembering the time she fell through the bed or something else as silly.

Dear Nand, you are always with me, looking over my shoulder and I miss you every day. You are the definition of Girl Power and I am so glad I got to take you on the journey in some way.

Well there you have it, everything I want to say on the whole matter from start to end.

It's my life or it was my life, I suppose with selling the collection off comes the task of looking for life's next challenge, I don't know what that will be yet but I know it will always be influenced in some way by the powerful women who have influenced and shaped my life.

Girl Power makes the world go round, without women there are no children and without children there is no future, it's that simple really.

Thank You

It's really strange to be writing a chapter of thank yous and of course this will be the hardest one to write, how do you even begin to tell people how grateful you are for their support. For their loyalty, hard work and passion as well as their dedication of time and effort to help you follow your dream. It's very humbling.

Dear Mum,

I don't know how we got to a stage where I am nearly 40 years old, but I know for sure I wouldn't have got anywhere near it without your constant love and support. I've put you through the ringer on more than one occasion and yet there you are at my back ready to catch me when I fall. When I was a little boy, you were my saviour, you were the one that fought my corner and stuck up for me at every wrong turn I took. I miss watching Eurovision with Bucks Fizz and hope we can do it again with our scorecards soon.

Thank you for being my mum, thank you for looking after me and thank you for checking in to make sure

I am okay. Love you more.

Dear Grandad,

I don't know where to begin or what to say to you, you have literally changed my way of thinking about life, the way I react to things and the way I treat people. I don't know how you do it, but you are a very natural mentor and I am hanging about for the foreseeable to learn a bit more. Plus, we do behave like naughty teenagers when out on the ran dan together, so we need to have some more of that fun please.

Thank you for believing in me and for encouraging me to follow me dreams, not only that but you put your hand in your own pocket to help me out and I will never ever forget that you took a risk on me!

Nand leaving has left us all a bit shell-shocked, standing back and watching you with your family, your little girl Ruby (Wonder Woman) and your little boy Max, and of course Judey Pants. You are an incredible man, you have more strength and determination than anyone I have ever known, and I hope you know just how proud of you Nand would be. I don't get to say that often but here it is in writing, it's true and I love you all the world.

I wish you would wear more pink and glitter occasionally but other than that I am so chuffed to have you as my best straight boy bestie.

Love you Grandad x

Dear Alex and Alex

You both came into my world through working on the exhibition, firstly Alex Maughan in Cyprus and then Alex Lodge a bit later. The input and the support that both of you have given to this project and to me had been unfaltering and I can't thank you both enough, I really couldn't have done it without either of you.

We made an amazing team of creatives and nothing made me happier than seeing you both enjoying yourselves at the launch evenings looking absolutely fabulous as always.

You were both capable of telling me to fuck off when you needed to or telling me not to be so stupid with some sort of mad idea.

I'm sorry we can no longer work together as a creative team, I feel like I have let you both down a lot, I know that times have been tough, especially at the end but hopefully one day you will be able to look back with a lot of fondness for what we did achieve and not focus on what went wrong at the end.

Alex M, I will never stop fighting to get you an apology, I don't know any gentleman in this world that wouldn't apologise to you for the way that you were treated on the last evening of London, the people involved should be utterly ashamed of their behaviour and I will not rest until you have an official sorry.

I love you both dearly xx

Dear Steven,

Wow, what a journey eh? How did that happen? Where have the last two years of our lives gone?

I don't even know where to begin saying sorry but then I know you would tell me instantly there is no need. We are always a team, always in it together and this was no different. We tried our absolutely hardest, but it wasn't meant to be.

What I did learn is that you are even more incredible than I ever had given you credit for. You are so head strong and determined it is crazy. You are bloody pig-headed but that pig-headedness allows you to do absolutely anything you set your mind to.

The exhibition nearly killed you and I am sorry that I put you through that. I could see the pain on your face and I never want to see you looking like that again.

It's time to go back to basics baby, me, you and an everyday normal(ish) lifestyle, quality time together, some downtime and general appreciation of you as a person.

I've never loved anyone the way that I love you and

quite simply I can't wait to spend the rest of my life with you. Without an exhibition!

I love you all the world Mr TV xxx

Other thanks to:

The Spice Girls – For teaching me to believe in myself

Jennifer – For being my best friend since I was 12 years old, how did we get to be this grown up?

Georgia – For having my back at the exhibition and making me laugh on a daily basis….Boooyah

Josh – For being a handsome bugger, making me smile and being a mate oh and for box lifting skills.

To all the team who helped – Lucy, Matt, Seth, Harry, Sarah, Dane, Adam, and everyone else who helped man the desks at the exhibitions, you were the face of the show and people always loved you.

The last mention has to go to you, the reader of this book, the visitors of the exhibition and the Spice Girls' fans that travelled from all over the world. You are what made it all worth it, to see die hard Spice Girls' fans walk into an exhibition, sometimes skip or dance in, and then come out telling us how much they loved it. How much it made them remember their childhood with their friends or their sisters or family.

One thing the Spice Girls have always had is the feel-good factor and their fans are exactly the same. It was truly my pleasure to meet every single person that I could and did at the exhibition, to hear that the Spice Girls had the same impact on so many other people's lives as they had on me.

It really is a Spiceworld and Spiceworld is bloody fantastic, thank you all for the support I hope I did you proud.

Alan xx

Printed in Great Britain
by Amazon